Cool Japan

The Book of
Basic Japanese
Cooking

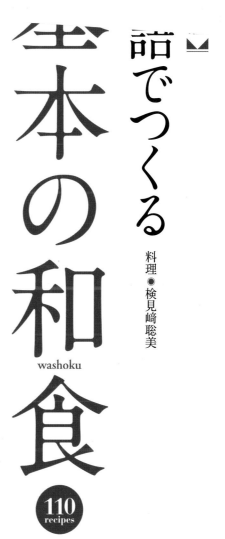

英語でつくる

基本の和食

料理◉検見﨑聡美

washoku

110 recipes

主婦の友社

CONTENTS

PART8 卵・豆腐・その他
Eggs, Tofu and More

本書の使い方

▶ 使用する小さじ1は5ml、大さじ1は15ml、1カップは200mlです。ただし米は1カップを180mlとして計算しています（p23）。

▶ 大さじはtablespoonを省略してtbsp、小さじはteaspoonを省略してtspと表記します。

▶ できあがりの分量は目安です。

▶ だしは、かつおだしです（p24）。

▶ 英文は、日本語のレシピの対訳となっていますが、逐語訳ではなくネイティブにわかりやすいように訳しました。

How to use this book

▶ One teaspoon is 5ml, one tablespoon is 15ml, and one cup is 200ml. However, the cup used for rice is 180ml (see page 23).

▶ Tablespoon and teaspoon are abbreviated as tbsp and tsp, respectively.

▶ Quantities described in the recipes are estimations.

▶ Soup stock refers to dried bonito soup stock (see page 24).

▶ The English is a translation of the Japanese recipes. The English is translated to make it easy for non-Japanese to understand and is not a word-for-word translation.

1月 JANUARY

おせち料理

Osechi-ryori (New Year's Foods)

お正月のごちそう

お正月にはおせち料理を食べます。本来、おせち料理というのは、正月七日、上巳の節句、端午の節句、七夕、重陽の五節句の際に備える料理全般をさしていました。そのうち、節句のうちでも、特に重要な正月の料理だけを「おせち料理」と呼ぶようになったのです。

正月のおせちは、1年の家内安全と無病息災を願うものです。そのため、材料も内容も、語呂合わせで縁起をかつぐものが多くなっています。

いずれも保存がきく料理にし、松の内はおせち料理以外は食べないとされていました。これは、年神様を迎え

Festive foods for Shogatsu (New Year's)

People eat osechi-ryori on New Year's. In the olden days, osechi-ryori referred to the festive food served on the first seven days of the New Year, Joshi-no-sekku (Peach Festival), Tango-no-sekku (Boys' Day), Tanabata (Star Festival), and Choyo-no-sekku (Chrysanthemum Festival). Because New Year's is the most important of all celebrations, the term osechi-ryori is now used to refer only to New Year's foods.

Osechi-ryori is offered as a prayer for the safety and good health of the household and its members throughout the year. For this reason, the names of many of the ingredients and contents have special meanings.

Most of the dishes in osechi-ryori can be preserved throughout the first seven days of the New Year, so people did not eat anything else but osechi-ryori during that time. The rationale behind this custom was to avoid using fire while the gods of the year were present.

Osechi-ryori is packed in special lacquered boxes called

ている間は煮炊きを慎むという意味です。

　おせちを詰める重箱は、外が黒、中が赤のものが正式です。伝統的なおせちは四段重ねです。

◉一の重・・・口取り
◉二の重・・・焼き物
◉三の重・・・煮物
◉四の重・・・酢の物

「四」は「死」につながると避けられ「与」の字を使うのが普通です。それぞれのお重には、三品、五品、七品など料理の種類を奇数にして、四隅をあけないように詰めます。

jubako. The outsides of the boxes are lacquered black and the insides have red lacquer. A traditional jubako set for osechi-ryori has four tiers.

◉ Ichino-ju(first box) → sweet hors d'oeuvres
◉ Nino-ju (second box) → grilled items
◉ Sanno-ju(third box) → stewed items
◉ Yono-ju(fourth box) → vinegared foods

　The fourth box is called yono-ju (「与の重」). The character yo is used instead of the number four (「四」) which has the same sound as the word shi (death). When packing the jubako, each box should contain an uneven number of items such as three, five, or seven items, making sure that the boxes are filled to all the corners without leaving any vacant space.

お雑煮

Ozoni

地方によって千差万別

　もともとは、年末に年神様にお供えしたもちや大根、にんじんなど、さまざまな供物を、元旦に下げ、「若水」で煮て皆で食べたのが始まりといわれています。

　現代でも正月の祝い膳には欠かせないものですが、土地や家によって材料や調理法は千差万別です。大きく分けると、①すまし汁仕立て(関東、中国、九州など)②白みそ仕立て(関西など)③小豆雑煮(東北、中国、九州の一部など)の三つの方法があります。

Each region has its own recipe.

　Originally, ozoni was a way of using the offerings made to gods at the year end, such as mochi (rice cakes), daikon radish, carrots, and other foods, by cooking them in wakamizu (the first water drawn from the well on New Year's day).

　Ozoni is an essential item for New Year's, even today. Each region and each household has its own recipes. Ozoni can be categorized into three main groups, namely clear soup base (Kanto, Chugoku, and Kyushu regions), white miso base (Kansai region), and red bean base (Tohoku, Chugoku, part of Kyushu).

ひな祭り

Hina-matsuri (Doll Festival)

女の子のお祭り

　3月3日のひな祭りは、女の子の美しい成長と幸福を願うものです。ひな祭りは「桃の節句」「弥生の節句」ともいわれますが、もともとは五節句の一つ、「上巳の節句」でした。

　この日は、古代中国では忌日とされ、その穢れを祓うため、水辺の行事を催す習俗がありました。それが、平安期ごろに日本に伝わり、紙で人形を作り、自分の身がわりとして穢れを移し、川や海に流すようになったのです。当時の幼女たちは、紙の人形で遊ぶことを「ひいな遊び」と言っていたことから「ひな人形」と呼ぶようになりました。

　ひな人形を段飾りにして、美しく飾って祝うようになったのは、江戸時代になってからです。もっとも、そのような形でお祝いを行ったのは、武家や貴族などだけでした。慣習が一般家庭に定着したのは、明治以後のことです。

Girls' Day

　Hina-matsuri, March 3, is a day to pray for the beauty and happiness of young girls. Hina-matsuri is also referred to as Momono-sekku (Peach Festival) or Yayoino-sekku (March Festival). It was originally called Joshino-sekku and was one of the five major festivals of the year.

　This day was considered an unlucky one in ancient China, so people held events near water for purification. During the Heian Period, this concept was adapted in Japan. It was believed that paper dolls put into rivers and oceans to float away would remove the evil and uncleanliness from oneself. Little girls used to play with paper dolls in what was called hiina-asobi, so the dolls were called hina dolls.

　It was during the Edo Period when hina dolls arranged on tiers became very elaborate and started to occupy prominent places in the homes of the rich and powerful warriors and aristocrats. After the Meiji Period, ordinary people started to adopt this custom.

4月 APRIL

花見

Hanami (Cherry Blossom Viewing)

桜を愛でて楽しむ

「花見」の歴史は、貴族が梅を見て楽しんだ奈良時代にさかのぼります。平安時代になると、梅よりも桜に人気が集まるようになりました。平安京の紫宸殿の前には桜が植えられ、宮中の人々は桜を楽しみました。

鎌倉時代からは、嵐山が桜の名所となり、各地に桜が植えられて名所が数多く誕生しました。江戸時代になって徳川吉宗が江戸の各所に桜を植え、花見の習慣が庶民に広まりました。桜は3月の下旬から4月上旬にかけて満開になります。花が命を繋ぐのはわずか2週間ほどで「はかない美しさ」の象徴にもよく使われます。

花見のときに飲む酒を花見酒といい、夜に桜を楽しむことを「夜桜見物」といいます。

Enjoying the cherry blossoms

The history of hanami goes back to the Nara Period, when aristocrats enjoyed viewing plum blossoms. During the Heian Period, cherry blossom viewing also became popular. Members of the imperial court enjoyed viewing the cherry trees that were planted in front of the Heiankyo Shishin Imperial Palace.

Since the Kamakura Period, Arashiyama has been famous for cherry blossoms. Cherry trees were planted in different places, creating many famous viewing spots. During the Edo Period, the shogun Yoshimune Tokugawa planted flowering cherry trees all over Edo (now Tokyo), turning hanami into a popular form of recreation for ordinary people. Cherry blossoms come out towards the end of March and are in full-bloom in early April. The flowers may be enjoyed for only two short weeks, and they are often used as symbols of transient beauty. The sake served during hanami is called hanami-zake. Appreciating the cherry blossoms at night is called yozakura-kenbutsu.

こどもの日

Kodomono-hi (Children's Day)

こどものお祭り

5月5日は、男の子のお祭り「端午の節句」です。また、男女を問わず、子どもの健やかな成長と幸福を願う「こどもの日」でもあります。古代中国では5月を物忌みの月とし、中でも5が重なる5月5日を特別な日と考えて、邪気を祓うさまざまな行事を行ってきました。この風習が日本に伝わり、奈良時代にはよもぎや菖蒲で厄よけをするならわしができました。鎌倉時代には菖蒲が転じて武事を尊ぶ「尚武」の催しとなり、江戸時代には、男の子の出世を願う行事として定着したのです。

Children's Festival

May 5 is Tangono-sekku (Boys' Day). It is also called Children's Day, a day to pray for the health, growth and happiness of boys and girls. In ancient China, the fifth month of the year was considered unlucky. May 5 was even worse because there are two fives in the date. So, many religious events were carried out on this day in order to drive away evil spirits. The custom arrived in Japan and people started a tradition of using yomogi (mugwort) and shobu (iris) leaves to protect themselves from evil during the Nara Period. During the Kamakura Period, a homonym of shobu meaning "honoring the way of the sword," was adopted. The significance of the day gradually changed, and by the Edo Period it had become an event to pray for the success of young boys.

七夕

Tanabata (Star Festival)

ロマンチックな年に一度の逢瀬

七夕は、中国から伝わった伝説や風習と、日本古来の信仰が結びついて生まれたものです。

- 7月7日の夜に、牽牛星が天の川を渡って織女星との年に1度の逢瀬を楽しむという、ロマンチックな説話。

The Yearly Romantic Rendezvous of Two Stars

This event is a hybrid of Chinese legends and customs with indigenous Japanese religious beliefs:

- A romantic story about the star Altair crossing the Milky Way to meet with the star Vega once a year on July 7.
- An event called kikoden, in which a maiden

◉ 女性が裁縫の上達を願い、さおの先に五色の糸
をかけて祈った「乞巧奠」
◉ 若い女性が機織り小屋にこもって神を迎え、村人
の穢れを祓う「棚機つ女」の信仰

などが重なり合って、現在の七夕祭りの原型が生まれたとされています。平安の宮廷貴族の時代には、すでに短冊に詩歌や願い事を書いて竹に結び、祈るという風習ができていました。

現在の七夕飾りは、五色の短冊に、願い事を書き、笹竹につるします。前日6日の夕方に軒先に飾り、7日の夜にとり込むのが正式な方法です。

would pray for weaving skills by hanging five colored threads on the tip of a bamboo stick.

◉ A religious belief called tanabata-tsume, which involved a maiden shutting herself in a weaving hut to receive gods in order to rid the villagers of impurity.

From these ideas was born the original form of Tanabata (Star Festival). During the Heian Period, aristocrats used to write poems and wishes on pieces of paper and hang them from bamboo branches.

Today, people write wishes on strips of paper of five different colors and hang them from bamboo. The bamboo is placed under the eaves on the evening of July 6 and are taken inside at night on July 7.

お盆

Obon (Bon Festival)

ご先祖様が帰ってくる

お盆というのは、7月15日を中心に行われる先祖供養の仏教行事です。しかし、現在は、一般的に8月13~16日の4日間(地方によっては15日まで)を「お盆」といっています。お盆には先祖の霊を迎えるための「精霊棚」(盆棚、先祖棚などともいう)をつくります。お供えもの、お水、線香、野菜でつくった動物などを供えます。きゅうりの馬やなすの牛をつくるのは、先祖の霊は馬に乗り、牛に荷物を引かせて帰ってくると考えられていたからです。

The Ancestors Return

Obon is a Buddhist event that takes place around July 15. In most areas, obon is held from August 13 to 16, while in other areas, it is held from August 13 to 15. During obon, shoryodana (spirit altars, also known as bondana or senzodana) are made to welcome back ancestors. Offerings, water, incense, and animals made with vegetables are offered to the spirits. People make horses with cucumbers or cows with eggplants because it is thought that the ancestors' spirits can ride the horses, and that the cows can help them carry their belongings.

お月見

Otsukimi (Moon-viewing)

月が一番美しい季節

　9月の満月の日は、月見の日とされています。中国では、古くから旧暦の7月を初秋、8月を仲秋、9月を晩秋と呼び、その月の満月の夜には、月見の宴を催すならわしがありました。中でも、旧暦8月15日の夜は「十五夜」と呼ばれました。その夜の月は、1年中で最も明るく美しい「仲秋の名月（明月）」として、季節の果物や花を供え、月をめでる「お月見」の行事が行われました。

　この雅やかなならわしは、平安時代に貴族の間に広がり、江戸時代には、庶民社会にも定着しました。そして、ただ月を鑑賞するだけではなく、農作物などの収穫物を供えて月を祭る性格の行事になりました。

The Season for Seeing the Moon at Its Best

　The night of the full moon in September is otsukimi (moon-viewing). In China, July on the lunar calendar was called Shoshu, while August and September were called Chushu and Banshu respectively. On the night of the full moon in these months, it was customary to have a moon-viewing banquet. The night of August 15 on the lunar calendar was called Jugoya (the 15th night). The moon that night was considered the brightest of the entire year and was appreciated as Chushu-no-meigetsu (the brightest and most beautiful moon in August on the lunar calendar). Many offerings of seasonal fruits and flowers were made, and people enjoyed otsukimi (moon-viewing).

　This elegant event became very popular among members of the aristocracy during the Heian Period. In the Edo Period, it became a popular celebration among the masses. It was a night not only to view and appreciate the moon, but also to pray to the moon with offerings of the harvest from the fields.

10月11月 OCTOBER NOVEMBER

七五三

Shichi-go-san(7-5-3)

子供たちの祝いの日

　11月15日は「七五三」です。男の子は数え年の3歳と5歳、女の子は3歳と7歳になると、氏神様に参拝して、子どもの無事な成長を感謝し、将来の幸せを祈るという行事です。

Festival Day for Children

　November 15 is Shichi-go-san (7-5-3). It is a day to give thanks for health and pray for guardian gods for the future happiness of three-and five-year-old boys, and three-and seven-year-old girls.

当時は子どもの死亡率も高く、「七つ前は神の子」という言葉があるように、7歳までは社会の一員として認められず、罪もとがめられず、喪に服することもありませんでした。七五三は、幼児期の大事な節目をつつがなく迎えられたことを祝い、また、社会の一員になったことを披露する意味もあったわけです。

In the old days, the mortality rates of young children being so high, children were thought to belong to the gods until the age of seven. A child younger than seven years old was not considered a full-fledged member of society. They were not punished for their sins and did not have to mourn. The Shichi-go-san festival was an important event to mark turning points during infancy, and to show one had become a member of society.

12月 DECEMBER

大みそか

Omisoka (New Year's Eve)

1年の締めくくり

みそかというのは、各月末のことです。1年の最後の日である12月31日は特に「大みそか」といいます。以前は、前日の30日までに、正月準備や飾りつけなどはすべてすませるのがならわしでした。大みそかは心身を清め、神社にこもるなどして、眠らずに年神様を迎える風習がありました。

夜には年越しそばを食べます。これは江戸時代に始まった習慣で、もともとは大みそかの夜の祝い膳の一つでした。今日では、そばが細く長いことにあやかり、延命や幸せが長く続くことを願う縁起物となりました。

The End of the Year

Misoka means the end of the month. December 31, being the last day of the year, is called Omisoka, meaning "large" or "great" misoka. All the preparation for New Year's had to be completed by December 30 so that people could cleanse themselves and wait for the spirits, staying up all night in the shrine on December 31.

At night, people eat toshikoshi-soba (year-end buckwheat noodles). The custom of eating noodles started during the Edo Period. Buckwheat noodles used to be one of the dishes eaten during year-end festivities, and the long, thin shape of buckwheat noodles symbolize long life and continued happiness.

関東風雑煮
KANTO STYLE ZONI SOUP

すまし汁に焼いた四角いもちが特徴。
Grilled square mochi in a clear broth.

159 kcal
1人分
One serving

材料（2人分）

切りもち …………………………2個
大根………(5mm 厚さの輪切り) 4枚
にんじん …(5mm 厚さの輪切り) 2枚
小松菜 …………………………30g
紅白のかまぼこ…(1cm 厚さ) 各2枚
ゆずの皮 ……………………… 少々
だし ………… 2½カップ (500ml)
塩………………小さじ¼ (1.25ml)
みりん ……………… 小さじ1 (5ml)
しょうゆ ……………………… 少々

作り方

1. 大根は、2枚は大きめの菊の抜き型で抜き、2枚は小さめの梅の抜き型で抜く。にんじんも梅の型で抜く。大根とにんじんはだし1カップでやわらかく煮、汁けをきる。小松菜は色よくゆでて水にとり、3cm長さに切って2等分し、そろえて水けをしぼる。

2. もちは半分に切り、オーブントースター（または焼き網）でこんがりと焼く。

3. だし1½カップを一煮立ちさせ、塩、みりんで味をつけ、しょうゆを加えて香りを添える。

4. 器に①の菊型の大根を敷き、その上に焼いたもちを盛り、①の他の野菜と紅白のかまぼこを彩りよく盛り添える。

5. ゆずの皮の黄色い表面を薄くそいでのせ、熱い③の汁を注ぐ。

Ingredients (2 servings)

2 pieces of kirimochi (rectangular dried mochi)
4 daikon radish slices (5mm thick)
2 carrot slices (5mm thick)
30g komatsuna greens
Red and white fish paste slices (1cm thick), 2 each
Yuzu citrus rind, to your taste
2 ½ cups (500ml) soup stock
¼ tsp (1.25ml) salt
1 tsp (5ml) mirin (sweet sake)
Soy sauce, to your taste

Directions

1. Cookie-cut 2 daikon radish slices using a large chrysanthemum-shaped cutter. Use a smaller plum-shaped cutter for the other 2 daikon radish slices and the 2 carrot slices. Simmer the daikon radish and carrots in 1 cup of soup stock until tender. Drain well. Boil komatsuna greens until color changes and remove. Cut into lengths of 3cm and divide into 2 equal parts. Squeeze well.

2. Cut the kirimochi in half and grill in a toaster oven (or oven grill) until browned.

3. Bring 1 ½ cups of soup stock to a boil. Season with salt, mirin, and add soy sauce.

4. Lay the daikon radish chrysanthemums in a bowl and place the grilled mochi on top. Serve garnished with plum-shaped vegetables from 1 and fish paste.

5. Thinly shave off yellow yuzu citrus rind and place it on top. Pour on the hot broth from 3.

ちらしずし
CHIRASHI-ZUSHI

ひなまつりに楽しみたい。
A hina-matsuri treat.

562 kal
1人分
One serving

材料（2人分）

米		2 カップ (360ml)
れんこん		100g
にんじん		1本
卵		2個
あなご（刻んだもの）		100g
昆布		4cm角を1枚
酒		大さじ2 (30ml)
A	酢	大さじ4 (60ml)
	砂糖	大さじ1 (15ml)
	塩	小さじ1 (5ml)
B	だし	½カップ(100ml)
	砂糖	小さじ1 (5ml)
	しょうゆ	大さじ½(7.5ml)
	塩	少々
木の芽		適宜

作り方

1. 炊飯器に米を入れ、目盛りまで水を入れる。大さじ4（60ml）の水をすくい出して酒をまぜ、昆布をのせて炊く。

2. Aの酢、砂糖、塩を合わせて、砂糖と塩をよくとかしておく。

3. れんこんは薄いいちょう切りにして水にさらし、水けをきる。にんじんは3cm長さの細切りにする。

4. なべにBを合わせて、れんこん、にんじんを入れ、ほとんど汁けがなくなるまで全体をまぜながら煮る。

5. とき卵をフライパンに入れて火にかけ、菜箸4〜5本で手早くかきまぜてポロポロになるまで火を通す。

6. ごはんは大きめのボウルに移す。すし酢をしゃもじに受けて回しかけ、大きくまぜて全体に行き渡らせる。

7. かたくしぼったぬれぶきんをかけて、そのまま10分蒸らし、すし酢を吸収させる。

8. うちわであおぎながら大きく切るようにまぜて、余分な水分をとばし、人肌程度に冷ます。

9. すしめしに具を広げてのせ、さっくりまぜる。器に盛り、木の芽をあしらう。

作る前にしておくこと / Before getting started

米は炊く30分前にといで、
ざるに上げておく。

Rinse out the rice 30 minutes before cooking and put it in a strainer.

Ingredients (2 servings)

2 cups (360ml) rice
100g lotus root
1 carrot
2 eggs
100g conger eel (chopped)
1 piece kobu seaweed (4×4cm square)
2 tbsp (30ml) sake

A | 4 tbsp (60ml) vinegar
 | 1 tbsp (15ml) sugar
 | 1 tsp (5ml) salt

B | ½ cup (100ml) soup stock
 | 1 tsp (5ml) sugar
 | ½ tbsp (7.5ml) soy sauce
 | Salt, to your taste

Leaf buds, as needed

Directions

1. Put the rice into a rice cooker and fill with water to the appropriate level. Take out 4 tbsp (60ml) of water, add the sake, put in the kobu, and cook.

2. Combine all the ingredients in A and dissolve the sugar and salt.

3. Slice the lotus roots into thin slices, and then into quarters. Soak in water and drain. Cut the carrots into thin uniform slices 3cm long.

4. Combine the ingredients in B in a pot, add the lotus root and carrot, then stir and cook until most of the liquid has been cooked out.

5. Heat the frying pan and add the beaten eggs. Stir quickly using 4 or 5 large chopsticks and cook until the eggs are scrambled well.

6. Transfer the rice into a big bowl. Drizzle the sushi vinegar onto the rice paddle and all over the rice. Mix well.

7. Cover with a well wrung-out cloth, and let the cooked rice sit for 10 minutes to soak some of the sushi vinegar.

8. With a hand fan, fan out the excess moisture and cool the rice to body temperature by stirring with cutting strokes.

9. Spread the main ingredients onto the sushi rice and mix lightly. Serve garnished with leaf buds.

ボウルのかわりに、
あれば盤台で
You can use a handai wooden tub instead of a bowl.

ぼたもち
AZUKI BEAN MOCHI

たっぷりのあんで包んだ、お彼岸に欠かせない和菓子。

Wrapped in plenty of red beans, this is a Japanese sweet not to be missed during Ohigan (the spring and fall equinoxes)!

104 kcal
1個分
One portion

Ingredients (24 pieces)

A | 1 cup (180ml) mochi-gome (glutinous rice)
  | 1 cup (180ml) rice

About ¼ cup (50ml) boiling water
600g red bean paste (store-bought variety)

Directions

1. Combine and rinse the regular and mochi rice in A. Drain in a strainer for 20 minutes. Place in a rice cooker and fill with water to the graduated mark 2 and cook. While still hot, use a wooden mallet or other tool to crush half the rice. Add the boiling water a little at a time to control the consistency of the rice. When it's sticky enough for mochi, divide it into 24 balls while still hot.

2. Divide the red bean paste into 24 parts (25g each) and lightly roll into balls. Squish them lightly in your palm and put 1 in the middle.

3. Stretch the red bean paste around the rice and pinch it shut on the bottom. Smooth the shape.

材料（24個分）

A | もち米‥‥‥‥1カップ（180ml）
  | 米‥‥‥‥‥‥1カップ（180ml）

熱湯‥‥‥‥‥約¼カップ（50ml）
粒あん（市販品）‥‥‥‥‥‥600g

作り方

1. Aの米は合わせてとぎ、ざるに上げて20分おく。炊飯器に入れて「2」の目盛りまで水を加えて炊き上げる。熱いうちにすりこ木などで突いてごはんを半分潰す。このとき、熱湯を少しずつ加えてごはんの固さを調節しながら突き、粘りけのあるもち状になったら、熱いうちに24等分して丸める。

2. あんは24等分（1個25g）して軽く丸め、手のひらにのせて軽くつぶし、①をまん中にのせる。

3. あんをのばすようにしてごはんを包み込む。あんのとじ目を下にして、形をととのえる。

月見だんご
MOON-VIEWING DUMPLINGS

十五夜のお月見に飾る伝統の蒸し菓子。

A traditional steamed cake to accompany viewing the full moon.

48 kcal

1個分
One portion

Ingredients (15 portions)

200g top-grade rice flour
About ¾ cup (150ml) water

Directions

1. Knead the rice flour while adding luke-warm water until the dough has the consistency of your ear lobe.

2. Place a damp cloth in a steamer and tear 1 into 5 to 6 pieces. Arrange and steam them on high for 20 minutes until warm in the center.

3. Get another damp cloth to knead the dough with because it's very hot. Knead until springy and glossy. If the dough gets hard, add some water to keep it at the consistency of your ear lobe.

4. Divide the dough into 15 pieces and roll into balls. Line a steamer with parchment paper and line the bottom with 8 balls, place 4 on top of them, and then 2 more, followed by 1 ball at the very top.

5. Steam on high for 15 minutes. Remove them while still hot and cool with a paper fan. They will become glossy when cool.

材料 (15個分)

上新粉 ……………………… 200g
ぬるま湯 …… 約¾ カップ (150ml)

作り方

1. 上新粉にぬるま湯を加えながらねり、耳たぶ程度のかたさの生地にする。

2. 蒸し器にかたく絞ったぬれぶきんを敷き、①を5〜6つにちぎって並べ、強火で20分蒸して中まで火を通す。

3. 新しいぬれぶきんにとり出し、とても熱いので、ふきんを使ってこねる。まとまったらさらに弾力とつやが出るまでこねる。生地がかたいようなら水少々を加え、耳たぶ程度のかたさにする。

4. ③を15等分してだんごに丸める。クッキングペーパーを敷いた蒸し器にだんごを8個並べ、その上に4個、その上に2個、最後に1個と積み重ねる。

5. 強火で15分蒸す。熱々をとり出し、うちわであおいで冷ましてつやを出す。

年越しそば
TOSHI-KOSHI SOBA (YEAR-END BUCKWHEAT NOODLES)

そばの持つ風味を味わうなら、まずはつゆだけでどうぞ。そのあとは好みの薬味で楽しんで。

To enjoy the flavor of soba, first try it with just the soy sauce noodle soup. After that, enjoy it with your favorite seasonings.

382 kal
1人分
One serving

材料（2人分）

そば（乾めん）……………………150g
焼きのり ……………………… ½枚
めんつゆ ………………………… 適宜
大根 …………………………… 150g
あらびき黒こしょう…………… 少々
たくあん ……………………… 20g
すり白ごま …………… 小さじ1 (5ml)
にら ……………………………2本
くるみ ………………………… 適宜
梅肉…………………… 大さじ½ (7.5ml)

作り方

1. めんつゆは冷やしておく。のりは細
切りにする。

2. 薬味3種を用意する。大根はすりお
ろしてざるに入れ、自然に水気をき
ってあらびきこしょうをまぜる。たく
あんは細切りにし、すりごまであえる。
にらは小口切りにし、くるみは小さく
割って梅肉であえる。

3. 別のなべにたっぷりの湯を沸かし、
そばを表示どおりにゆでる。ざるに
とって冷水で洗い、水けをよくきる。

4. 器にそばを盛り、のりをのせる。め
んつゆ、②の薬味を添える。

Ingredients (2 servings)

150g soba (dried noodles)
½ sheet roasted nori seaweed
Noodle dipping sauce,
as needed
150g daikon radish
Rough ground black pepper,
to your liking
20g pickled daikon radish
1 tsp (5ml) ground white sesame
2 garlic chives
Walnuts, as needed
½ tbsp (7.5ml) umeboshi meat

Directions

1. Chill the noodle dipping sauce.
Cut the nori seaweed into thin
strips.

2. Prepare the three condiments.
Grate the daikon radish and put
into a strainer. Let the liquid drain
out at its own speed, and then
mix with roughly ground pepper.
Slice the takuan pickles into thin
strips and mix with the ground
sesame seeds. Slice the garlic
chives thinly, crack the walnuts
into small pieces, and mix with
the umeboshi meat.

3. Bring a full pot of water to a boil
and cook the soba noodles as
instructed on the package. Put the
cooked soba in a strainer, rinse
with cold water, and drain well.

4. Place the noodles on a bamboo
soba dish and put the nori
seaweed on top. Add the
condiments from 2 to the dipping
sauce.

めんつゆ

基本のめんつゆは、だし、しょうゆ、み
りんの割合が4:1:1。一度煮立ててア
ルコール分をとばし、まろやかに。

材料

だし……………………200ml
しょうゆ ………………50ml
みりん……………………50ml

作り方

なべにすべての材料を合わせて火に
かけ、一煮立ちさせる。あら熱をとり、
冷蔵庫で冷やす。

※そばはもちろん、うどんつゆ、そうめん
つゆなどにも使えます。

Noodle Dipping Sauce

The basic ingredients in dipping sauce are soup stock, soy
sauce and mirin at a ratio of
4:1:1. Remove the alcohol and
mellow the flavor by heating
to a boil once.

Ingredients
200ml soup stock
50ml soy sauce
50ml mirin (sweet sake)

Preparations
Put all the ingredients in a pot and
bring to a boil. Let the heat escape,
and then cool in the refrigerator. The
noodle soup can also be used for
udon noodles (thick-flour noodles),
and somen (fine white noodles).

ごはんの炊き方
HOW TO COOK RICE

厚手のなべで、つやつや、ふっくら炊き上げる。
Use a thick pot for full-bodied rice with a glossy appearance.

252 kcal

1人分(150g)
One serving(150g)

米のはかり方と水かげん

米は1カップ＝1合＝180mlです。炊飯器付属の計量カップは180mlなのでスプーンの柄などですりきりに。200mlの計量カップを使うときは、真横から見て180mlの目盛りに合わせます。

水かげんは米の1.2倍

なべでじょうずにごはんを炊くには、水かげんが大切。そのためには、米を計量カップに押し込んだりしないで目盛りまで入れ、表面を平らにならして計ります。水は米の1.2倍（2割増し）用意します。

材料（一度に炊きやすい分量）

米………………………2合（360ml）
水…………2カップ（400ml）＋32ml

作り方

1. 大きめのボウルに米を入れて水を注ぎ、手早くかきまぜてすばやく水を捨てる。これを2〜3回繰り返す。

2. 水をひたひたに注ぎ、手のひらのふくらんだ部分で押すようにシャッシャッととぐ。水を注いですすぎ、水を捨てる。これをあと2回ほど繰り返す。

3. 水が白く濁らなくなったら、米をざるに上げて20分おき、水気をきる。

4. 厚手できっちりとふたのできるなべを用意し、③の米を入れ、計った水を注いで米の表面を平らにならしてふたをする。

5. ④を強火にかける。なべの中がグラグラと煮立ち、ふたの間から吹きこぼれてきたらすぐに弱火にし、15分炊く。途中でふたは開けないこと。

6. 強火で10秒加熱して余分な水けをとばし、火からおろして10分蒸らす。

7. 水でぬらしたしゃもじをなべ肌に沿って入れてごはんをはがし、端から大きくすくって返し、全体を切るようにほぐす。

Measuring rice and the suitable amount of water

One cup of rice is 1 go(180 ml). The measuring cups that come with rice cookers are 180 ml, so you can fill them with rice and use the handle of a spoon or other utensil to get a level cup of rice. When using a 200ml cup, measure the rice by looking at the 180ml mark directly from the side.

The water should be 1.2 times the amount of rice.
When using a pot to cook rice, it is important to have the right amount of water for the rice to turn out well.

Put the required amount of rice in the measuring cup without stuffing it in and level the surface. The water should be 1.2 times the amount of rice (20% more).

Ingredients (for an amount that is easy to cook at one time)

2 cups (360ml) rice
2 cups (400ml) + 32ml water

Directions

1. Put the rice into a large bowl, add water and quickly run your hand through the rice. Pour out the water and wash again 2 or 3 times.

2. Fill the bowl with water to the level of the rice. Use the fleshy part of your palm to knead the rice, washing the rice quickly by lightly pressing. Pour out the water and then rinse twice more.

3. When the water no longer turns cloudy, pour the rice into a strainer and leave for 20 minutes. This will drain rice.

4. Get a thick pot with a secure lid. Put the rice from step 3 into the pot, add the water and level the rice. Cover the pot.

5. Set 4 to high heat. As soon as the pot reaches a rolling boil and the water starts splashing out of the lid, turn the heat to low and cook for 15 minutes. Don't remove the lid while the rice is cooking.

6. Set to high heat for 10 seconds to get rid of excess water. Remove the pot from the cooker and leave for 10 minutes.

7. Wet a shamoji (flat rice paddle) and use it to scrape the rice from the sides of the pot. Scoop the rice with large movements, starting at the sides, and stir all the rice, making strokes through the rice to separate the grains.

だしのとり方

MAKING A DELICIOUS SOUP STOCK

和食はなんといってもだしが決め手。
洋風、中華風などほかの料理のスープにくらべると、
簡単においしいだしがとれます。
きちんととっただしを使って、いつもの料理を極上の味にしましょう。

The soup stock is everything in Japanese cuisine.
Compared to Western, Chinese and other types of cuisine, making a wonderful soup stock for Japanese dishes is easy.
Using a properly made stock will give you the best possible results.

★かつおだし

昆布のうまみをプラスした風味豊かなかつおだしは、すまし汁から煮物まで幅広く使えます。この本に出てくる「だし」はすべてこのだしでOK。

材料（2人分）

削りがつお ……………………… 15g
昆布 …………… 3×4cmを2枚（7g）
水 ………………… 4カップ（800ml）

作り方

1. 昆布はかたくしぼったぬれぶきんで表面の汚れを軽くふきとる（洗うとうまみが出てしまう）。

2. 昆布はうまみが出やすいように、キッチンばさみで2cm長さの切り込みを2カ所に入れる。

3. なべに分量の水と、昆布を入れて、昆布がふっくらともどるまで、15〜20分ほどおく。

4. 弱火にかけて煮立ち始めたら（なべの縁まわりからこまかい泡が出始める）、昆布をとり出す。

★ Dried-bonito soup stock

Dried-bonito soup stock along with savory umami from kobu seaweed is great in dishes ranging from clear broths to simmered entrées. You can use this in all the recipes in this book that call for soup stock.

Ingredients (2 servings)

15g shaved dried-bonito
Two 3 × 4cm pieces (7g) kobu seaweed
4 cups (800ml) water

Directions

1. Wipe the surface of the kobu seaweed with a well wrung-out damp towel. (Washing it would remove most of the savory umami.)

2. To make it easier for the umami to seep into the water, use kitchen scissors to cut 2 cm into the kobu in two spots.

3. Put the measured-out water into a pot with the kobu and let it sit for about 15 to 20 minutes until the kobu becomes soft.

4. Heat at a low temperature until it starts to simmer (small bubbles appear around the edge of the pot), then take out the kobu.

5. 強火にかけて、煮立ったら削りがつおを入れ、浮いているものは菜箸で沈め、すぐに火を止める。

6. しばらくおいて削りがつおが沈んだら、ぬらしたペーパータオルを敷いた万能こし器でこす（しぼらないこと）。

5. Turn the heat to high, and when the water starts to boil, put in the shaved dried bonito. When the bonito floats up, push it down with large chopsticks and then turn off the heat.

6. Let it set until the shaved dried bonito sinks. Strain with a wet paper towel on the bottom of a general-purpose strainer. (Do not squeeze out the bonito.)

★煮干しのだし

煮干しでとる素朴な味わいのだしは、みそ汁やめんつゆ、しっかり味の野菜の煮物などに向きます。

材料（2人分）

煮干し ……………………… 20g
水 ……………… 3.5カップ（700ml）

作り方

1. 煮干しは、苦みと生ぐさみが出る頭と腹わたをとり、縦に身を裂いて背骨をとる。大きいものはさらに縦に裂く。

2. なべに分量の水、煮干しの身のみを入れ、30分ほどおく。

3. 中火にかけて、煮立ったら火を弱めてアクをていねいにとり、10分ほど煮出す。

4. 火を止めて、ぬらしたペーパータオルを敷いた万能こし器でこす。

★ Soup stock from dried baby sardines

The rustic flavor of soup stock made with dried baby sardines is perfect for miso soup, noodle dipping sauce, and stewed vegetables with a distinct flavor.

Ingredients (2 servings)

20g dried baby sardines
3.5 cups (700 ml) water

Directions

1. Remove the bitter head and stomach of the dried sardines, slice vertically and remove the spine. Slice bigger fish again vertically.

2. Put the measured water in a pot. Add only the dried sardines and allow to set for about 30 minutes.

3. Turn on the heat to medium high, and after it starts to boil, turn the heat to low. Carefully remove the scum and decoct for 10 minutes.

4. Turn off the heat and strain using a strainer with a wet paper towel spread out inside of it.

豆腐とわかめのみそ汁

TOFU AND WAKAME SEAWEED MISO SOUP

どちらも火が通りやすい素材なので、みそを先にとき入れてから加えて煮立つ寸前に火を止めます。

Both tofu and wakame are easily cooked, so stir in the miso first then add. Turn the heat off just before the soup boils.

69 kcal

1人分
One serving

材料（2人分）

絹ごし豆腐……………½丁 (150g)
カットわかめ（乾燥）……………2g
だし……………1¾カップ (350ml)
みそ…………… 大さじ1.5 (22.5ml)

作り方

1. 豆腐は1.5cm のさいの目切りにする。わかめは水でもどし、水けをしぼる。

2. なべにだしを入れて火にかける。一煮立ちしたら、みそをだしでときのばして加える。

3. すぐに豆腐、わかめを加えて一煮する。

Ingredients (2 servings)

½ block (150g) silken tofu
2g cut wakame seaweed (dried)
1 ¾ cups (350ml) soup stock
1.5 tbsp (22.5ml) miso

Directions

1. Cut the tofu into 1.5cm square pieces. Reconstitute the wakame seaweed in water, then drain out the water.

2. Put soup stock in a pot and heat. When it starts to boil, stir the miso into the soup stock to dissolve it.

3. Quickly add the tofu and wakame seaweed and bring to a boil, then turn off.

みそはなめらかにときのばして
Gently stir in the miso.

市販のだしを使うときは

忙しいときは、市販の顆粒状や液体のだし、だしパックが強い味方になってくれます。使うときは、風味を生かすために仕上げに加えるのがおいしくするコツ。みそ汁ならみそを加える直前に。煮物なら使う分量の半分を煮始めるときに入れて、残りの半分は仕上げに。商品によって濃度や塩分量が違うのでラベルの表示どおりに使いましょう。ただし味が濃いことが多いので、必ず味見をして味をととのえるようにしましょう。

Using a commercial soup stock

When you are busy, granular or liquid soup stock from the market comes in handy. The best way to use it is to add it to the finished dish as a last-minute flavoring. For miso soup, put it in the hot water just before adding the miso. For simmered dishes, put in half the soup stock when it starts to boil, and the other half toward the end to finish. The concentration and salinity may differ by product, so follow the instructions on the package. However, most of these commercial soup stocks are salty, so always trust in your own tongue to flavor to your taste.

にぎりずし
NIGIRIZUSHI (HAND-FORMED SUSHI)

職人技をマスターして、我が家がお寿司屋さん。
Master the skills of a professional and turn your dining room into a sushi restaurant.

210 kcal
1人分
One serving

材料

すし飯（32 ページ参照）……　適宜
すし種（好みで）
刺し身用まぐろ・生食用いか・蒸しえび・酢じめのこはだ・厚焼き卵など
……………………………　適宜
おろしわさび……………………　適宜

作り方

1. すし飯は人肌程度のあたたかいものを用意する。すし種のまぐろ、いか、卵焼きは握りやすい大きさに切り、他のすし種と、とりやすいように、並べておく。おろしわさび、手酢（水と酢を同量合わせたもの）も用意する。

2. 握る前に手を軽く手酢で湿らせ、右手ですし飯を1個分（約15ｇ）とり、手の中で4～5回軽く転がしてまとめる。

3. 左手の指先ですし種をつまんでとり、手のひらを返して指の第2関節の上にのせ、右手の人差し指でわさびを塗る。

4. すし種の上にすし飯をのせ、左手親指ですしめしのまん中をぐっと押さえると同時に、右手親指と人差し指で上下を押さえ込む。

5. 右手人差し指ですし飯を軽く押さえ、左手を少し起こしてすしを指先の方に半回転させ、すし種を上にする。右手でつまんで元の位置に戻す。

6. 左手の親指ですし飯の上部を支え、右手の人差し指となか指ですし種を押さえて、しっかりと形をつけるように握る。

7. 右手の親指と人差し指ですしの両側を持って前後を入れ替え、同様に握る。もう一度前後を入れ替えて最初の向きにし、同様に握って仕上げる。

Ingredients

Vinegared rice (see page 32), as needed
Sushi ingredients, as desired
Sashimi tuna, sushi squid, steamed shrimp, gizzard shad marinated in vinegar, thick omelet, etc
Grated wasabi, as needed

Directions

1. Prepare warm (body temperature) vinegared rice. Cut the tuna, squid, omelet and other sushi ingredients into pieces that are easy to hold. Arrange all the ingredients such that they are easy to pick. Prepare also the grated wasabi and vinegared water (water and vinegar) for wetting the hands.

2. Before touching the rice, lightly dip your hands into the vinegared water and use your right hand to take enough vinegared rice for one nigirizushi (about 15 g). Gently roll the rice in your hand 4 to 5 times to shape it.

3. Use the tips of the fingers of your left hand to pick sushi ingredients. Spread out your left hand and place the ingredients on the second joint. Use your right index finger to take some wasabi and paste it on the sushi ingredients.

4. Put the vinegared rice on the sushi ingredients. While firmly pressing the vinegared rice at the center with your left thumb, use your right thumb and index finger to press the top and bottom ends of the vinegared rice.

5. Gently hold down the vinegared rice with your right index finger and turn it towards the tips of your fingers so that the sushi ingredients are on top. Hold it in your right hand and put it back in its original position.

6. Press the top part of the vinegared rice with your left thumb and use your right index finger and middle finger to hold down the sushi while you firmly squeeze it into shape.

7. Hold both sides of the sushi using your right thumb and right index finger and switch sides. Squeeze it the same way. Turn it over to its original position once again and gently squeeze it to finish.

ごはん・めん Rice and Noodles

29

太巻きずし

THICK SUSHI ROLLS (FUTOMAKI-ZUSHI)

具の分量は、少し多め。
のりに合わせて長さをそろえて並べると、うまくいきます。
Use a generous amount of filling ingredients.
It will turn out better if the filling is arranged to fit the size of the nori seaweed.

766 kcal
1本分
One roll

材料（2本分）

すし飯 (p.32)	‥‥ 米 1.5 合分 (270ml)	
高野どうふ	‥‥‥‥‥‥‥‥‥	2個
かんぴょう	‥‥‥‥‥‥‥‥‥	1.5m
卵	‥‥‥‥‥‥‥‥‥	3個
焼きあなご	‥‥‥‥‥‥‥‥	1尾分
三つ葉	‥‥‥‥‥‥‥‥‥	1束
桜でんぶ	‥‥‥‥‥‥‥‥	適宜
焼きのり	‥‥‥‥‥‥‥‥	2枚

A | だし ‥‥‥‥‥‥‥‥‥ 250ml
　| 塩 ‥‥‥‥‥‥‥‥‥‥ 少々
　| しょうゆ ‥‥‥‥ 大さじ½ (7.5ml)
　| みりん ‥‥‥‥‥ 大さじ½ (7.5ml)

しょうゆ ‥‥‥‥‥‥ 大さじ½ (7.5ml)

B | みりん ‥‥‥‥‥ 小さじ2 (10ml)
　| しょうゆ ‥‥‥‥ 小さじ½ (2.5ml)
　| 塩 ‥‥‥‥‥‥‥‥‥‥ 少々

サラダ油、塩 ‥‥‥‥‥‥‥ 各適宜
酢（手水用、p.32）‥‥‥‥‥ 少々

作り方

1. 高野どうふは表示どおりにもどし、水けをしぼる。

2. かんぴょうは水で洗い、たっぷりの塩でもむ。しんなりしたら塩を洗い落とす。熱湯でさっとゆでて湯をきり、なべに戻し入れ、たっぷりの水を注いで火にかけ、透き通るくらいまでゆで、湯をきる。

3. なべにAを入れて中火にかけ、①、②を入れて落としぶたをし、15分ほど煮る。高野どうふをとり出してしょうゆを加え、さらに汁けがなくなるまで煮る。それぞれ冷ましておく。

4. ボウルに卵を割りほぐし、Bを加えて
   まぜ、サラダ油を熱した卵焼き器に
   流し入れ、厚焼き卵を作る。

5. ③の高野どうふの煮汁を軽くしぼ
   り、1cm角の棒状に切る。③のか
   んぴょうをざるに上げ、汁けをき
   る。焼きあなご、厚焼き卵は棒状に切る。
   三つ葉は熱湯で色よくゆでる。

6. 太巻きずしの巻き方 (p.32)を参照し
   て巻き、包丁で食べやすく切る。

使う道具　Equipment

飯台

すし飯 (p.32)を
作るときの道具。
使う前に水に浸し
て水けを吸わせ、ふ
きんでふく。乾燥したまま使うと、木
肌が合わせ酢を吸い込み、すし飯も
くっついてしまう。使用後はすぐに水
か湯で洗い、じゅうぶんに乾かして
からしまうこと。

Handai wooden rice tub

A tub used to make vinegared
rice. Before using, let it soak in
water, and then wipe dry with a
cloth. Using while still dry will
cause the vinegar to seep into the
wood and the rice to stick to the
surface. After use, wash with
water and dry thoroughly before
putting away.

Ingredients (for 2 rolls)

Vinegared rice (see page 32) : 1.5 cups
(270ml) rice
2 blocks koya-dofu
1.5m kanpyo (gourd shavings)
3 eggs
1 grilled conger eel
1 bunch mitsuba trefoil
Sakura-denbu, as needed
*Ground seasoned codfish dried to make
flakes, sweetened with mirin, sometimes
colored with red food coloring.
2 sheets roasted nori seaweed

A | 250ml soup stock
  | Salt, to your taste
  | ½ tbsp (7.5ml) soy sauce
  | ½ tbsp (7.5ml) mirin (sweet sake)

½ tbsp (7.5ml) soy sauce

B | 2 tsp (10ml) mirin (sweet sake)
  | ½ tsp (2.5ml) soy sauce
  | Salt, to your taste

Salad oil, salt, as needed
Vinegar, to your taste (see page 32,
vinegar for the hands)

Directions

1. Reconstitute the koya-dofu as instructed on the package, and then squeeze out the moisture.

2. Wash the kanpyo with water and rub with lots of salt. When the kanpyo becomes soft, wash off the salt. Place briefly in boiling water, and then drain off the water. Put it back in the pot, fill the pot with water, and heat. Cook until the kanpyo starts to look transparent, and then drain off the water.

3. Put A ingredients in a pot and cook over medium heat. Add the koya-dofu and kanpyo, and put on a drop lid. Simmer for 15 minutes. Remove the koya-dofu, add the soy sauce, and then boil off the liquid. Let everything cool.

4. Crack an egg into a bowl, add B and stir. Pour the seasoned egg into a square egg-frying pan and cook to make a thick omelet.

5. Gently squeeze the liquid from the koya-dofu and cut into 1cm rod-shaped pieces. Put the kanpyo in a strainer and drain. Cut grilled conger eel and eggs cooked in 4 into sticks. Boil mitsuba trefoil to a nice color.

6. To wrap the sushi rolls, refer to the explanation for making futomaki-zushi on page 32 and cut into bite-size pieces.

使う道具　Equipment

巻きす

のり巻きをまくときに
使う道具。飯台同様、
使用後はすぐに洗っ
てじゅうぶんに乾かす。きちんと乾
いてからしまわないと、カビが発生
することも。巻くときは、ひもの結び
目があるほうを向こう側にしておく。

Maki-su (bamboo mat)

An item used to roll the sushi roll.
Just as with the tub, wash it
immediately after use, and let it
dry completely before putting it
away. If it is not completely dried,
mold might form on it. When
rolling, make sure the side with
the knots is on the side away from
you.

ごはん・めん
Rice and Noodles

太巻きずしの巻き方 ／ How to roll futomaki-zushi

手水（水に酢少々を加える）を用意し、巻きすをおいて焼きのりを1枚縦長におく（のりはつるつるした面を下にする）。すし飯の半量をのせ、向こう2cm、手前1cmほどを残して、両端までしっかり手ですし飯を広げる。このとき手水をつけながら作業するとよい。すし飯は押しつぶさず、のりにのせるように広げる。

Prepare some water with a little vinegar, to use when wetting the hands. Roll out the bamboo mat and put a sheet of nori seaweed lengthwise on it. (The shiny side of the nori seaweed should face downward.) Put half of the vinegared rice on the nori seaweed, leaving 2 cm on the far edge and 1 cm on the edge closest to you, and spread the rice to the edges with your hands. While doing this, dip your fingers in the vinegared water. Spread out the rice on the nori without smashing the rice.

すし飯の中央から手前に、かんぴょう（1回折り返して重ねる）、焼きあなご、高野どうふ、厚焼き卵、三つ葉、桜でんぶの順にのせる。具はのりの長さに合わせて切りながら並べ、平たくではなく、四角くまとめるように積む。

Moving from the center of the rice towards you, put on the kanpyo (stack folded once), grilled conger eel, koya-dofu, thick omelet egg, mitsuba trefoil, and sakura-denbu, in that order. Arrange these ingredients along the length of the nori, cutting as necessary. Make sure to place them in a square and not lay them out flat.

具を押さえながら、のりといっしょに手前の巻きすを持ち上げ、手前のすし飯の端と向こう側のすし飯の端を合わせるように持っていく。

While holding the ingredients in place, lift up the front of the bamboo mat and let it touch the other side of the mat.

両手で軽く形をととのえる（この段階ではのりの端が巻きすから少し見える状態）。上の巻きすを少し転がし、きっちり巻く。

Gently push the roll into shape. (The nori seaweed should be a little visible from the bamboo mat.) Roll the bamboo mat a little to tighten the roll.

両手で軽く押さえ、落ち着かせる。

Using both hands, lightly push the roll into shape.

巻きすをはずし、食べやすい大きさに切り分ける。このとき、1切れごとに包丁の刃をぬれぶきんでふくと、すし飯がくっつかずにきれいに切れる。

Remove the bamboo mat, and cut the roll into bite-size lengths. Wiping the blade of the knife with a wet cloth after each cut will keep the rice from sticking to the knife.

すし飯の作り方 ／ How to make vinegared rice

ごはんが冷めていると酢が全体に回らないので、炊きたてのアツアツのごはんに合わせ酢を加え、粘りが出ないように手早くまぜること。そして、うちわであおぎながら冷まし、水分をとばすことがポイントです。

When the rice is cold, it will be difficult to spread the vinegar evenly throughout the rice. Add vinegar when the rice is still hot, right after it has finished cooking. Mix quickly to prevent stickiness. It's important to then fan the rice and decrease the moisture.

材料（2～3人分）	Ingredients (2 to 3 servings)
米 ………… 2合（360ml）	2cups (360ml) rice
こぶ ……………… 5cm	5cm kobu seaweed
A 酢 …… 大さじ4（60ml）	A 4 tbsp (60ml) vinegar
塩 …… 小さじ1（5ml）	1 tsp (5ml) salt
砂糖 … 大さじ2（30ml）	2 tbsp (30ml) sugar

米は洗って水けをきる。炊飯器の内がまに入れ、目盛りまで水を加えて大さじ2杯分の水をとり除き、こぶを入れる。そのまま20分ほどおき、普通に炊く。

Wash and drain the rice. Place it in a rice cooker and add water to the specified level. Remove 2 tbsp of water and then add the kobu seaweed. Allow the rice to set for about 20 minutes and cook in the rice cooker as usual.

合わせ酢を作る。Aはまぜ合わせ、砂糖と塩をとかしておく。飯台に水を含ませ、ふきんで水けをふく。

Prepare the vinegar by mixing the A ingredients, dissolving the sugar and salt. Moisten the rice tub, then wipe dry with a towel.

①のごはんが炊き上がったらこぶをとり出し、なるべくごはんをくずさないようにして飯台にあける。大きく2～3回まぜ、②の合わせ酢をしゃもじに受けながら全体に回しかける。

When the rice is cooked, remove the kobu seaweed, and put the rice in the tub without disturbing it any more than necessary. Stir it 2 or 3 times with broad strokes, then pour the vinegar mixture 2 over the rice, using the rice paddle (shamoji) to receive and spread it.

大きく2～3回まぜ、全体に合わせ酢が行き渡ったらひとまとめにし、かたくしぼったぬれぶきんをかけて5～6分おいて蒸らし、ごはんに合わせ酢を吸収させる。

Stir it again 2 or 3 times with broad strokes, making sure the vinegar gets mixed evenly, and lump it together. Put a well wrung-out damp cloth over the rice and wait for 5 to 6 minutes to let the rice absorb the vinegar.

うちわであおぎながら、切るようにまぜて水分をとばす。人肌くらいに冷めればよい。

While fanning with a paper fan, make cutting strokes to stir the rice, letting off moisture. Allow the rice to cool at body temperature.

細巻きずし3種

THREE KINDS OF SMALL SUSHI ROLLS

太巻きにくらべて具が少ないので、グンと巻きやすくなります。
These are easier to roll up than futomaki-zushi because they have less filling.

鉄火巻き
red tuna
182 kcal
1本分
One roll

たくあん巻き
pickled daikon radish
154 kcal
1本分
One roll

きゅうり巻き
cucumber
157 kcal
1本分
One roll

ごはん・めん
Rice and Noodles

Ingredients (6 rolls)

Vinegared rice (see page 32) : 1.5 cups (270ml) rice
½ cucumber
40g pickled daikon radish
6 ao-jiso green perilla leaves
60g red tuna (for sashimi)
Diced banno-negi onions, to your taste
Roasted white sesame, to your taste
3 sheets roasted nori seaweed

Directions

1. Cut the cucumber into thin strips.

2. Coarsely chop the pickled daikon radish and tear the green perilla in half lengthwise.

3. Cut the tuna into mid-sized strips.

4. Cut the seaweed in half lengthwise.

5. Place the seaweed horizontally on a bamboo mat, place ⅙ (75 to 80g) of the rice on it, leaving 5 mm from the edge on the side closest to you and 1cm from the edge on the opposite side and spread it all the way to the edge of the remaining 2 sides. You can wet your hands with water containing vinegar to make spreading the rice easier.

6. Lay some cucumber between the middle of the rice and the side closest to you and sprinkle on some sesame. Roll it the same way as futomaki-zushi (see left page). Make another cucumber roll. Using the same method, roll 2 pickled daikon radish and ao-jiso green perilla rolls and 2 tuna and banno-negi onion rolls.

7. Cut each roll into bite-size pieces.

材料（6本分）

すし飯（p.32）
………… 米1.5合分（270ml）
きゅうり……………………½本
たくあん……………………40g
青じそ………………………6枚
まぐろの赤身（刺し身用）… 60g
万能ねぎの小口切り……… 少々
いり白ごま…………………少々
焼きのり……………………3枚

作り方

1. きゅうりはせん切りにする

2. たくあんはあらいみじん切りに、青じそは縦半分にちぎる。

3. まぐろは棒状に切る。

4. のりは縦半分に切る。

5. 巻きすの上に焼きのりを1枚横長におき、すし飯の⅙量（75～80g）をのせ、向こう1cm、手前5mmほど残して、両端までしっかりすし飯を広げる。このとき手水をつけながら作業するとよい。

6. すし飯の中央から手前にきゅうりをのせてごまを振り、太巻きずしの巻き方（左ページ）を参照して巻く。これをあともう1本作る。同様にして、具をたくあんと青じそにして2本、まぐろと万能ねぎにして2本作る。

7. それぞれ、食べやすい大きさに切り分ける。

いなりずし

INARI-ZUSHI (DEEP-FRIED TOFU STUFFED WITH VINEGARED RICE)

すし飯をそのまま詰めてもいいですが、しば漬けを加えると、カリカリとした食感が加わっています。

You can simply pack vinegared rice into the inari pocket, but adding shibazuke pickles creates a crispy texture and enhances the flavor.

194 kcal
1個分
1 portion

材料（6個分）

すし飯（p.32）……米1合分（180ml）
油揚げ……………………………… 3枚
しば漬け…………………………… 30g
いり白ごま………… 大さじ2（30ml）

A｜だし……………………………200ml
　｜砂糖……… 大さじ1.5（22.5ml）
　｜しょうゆ…… 大さじ1.5（22.5ml）
　｜みりん…………大さじ1（15ml）

作り方

1. 油揚げはまないたに縦長にしておき、菜箸を1本のせて端から端まで押し付けるようにしてまんべんなく転がす。横半分に切り、切り口に指を入れて広げ、破らないようにていねいに袋状に開く。

2. なべにたっぷりの湯を沸かし、①を入れて2〜3分ゆでて油抜きをする。湯をきってぬるま湯で洗い、両手で油揚げをはさんで水けをしぼる。

3. なべにAを入れて中火にかけ、煮立ったら②を広げ入れて落としぶたをし、汁けがほとんどなくなるまで20分ほど煮る。ざるに広げて汁けをきりながら冷まし、両手で油揚げをはさんで汁けを軽くしぼる。あとで詰めやすいように、口を半分ほど折り返しておく。

4. しば漬けはみじん切りにし、すし飯に加える。ごまを加えてさっくりとまぜ、6等分して軽く丸くにぎっておく。

5. ③の油揚げの中に④を入れ、しっかりと油揚げの角まで詰めて、軽くにぎって形をととのえる。

Ingredients (6 portions)

Vinegared rice (see page 32) : 1 cup (180ml) rice
3 slices abura-age (deep-fried tofu)
30g shibazuke pickles
2 tbsp (30ml) roasted white sesame

A｜200ml soup stock
　｜1.5 tbsp (22.5ml) sugar
　｜1.5 tbsp (22.5ml) soy sauce
　｜1 tbsp (15ml) mirin (sweet sake)

Directions

1. Place the abura-age lengthwise on a cutting board, put a single large chopstick on the abura-age and roll from one side to the other while pressing. Cut in half horizontally. Put your fingers into the cut and expand it, careful not to break through the surface, and make a pocket.

2. Bring a pot full of water to a boil and put in the abura-age for 2 or 3 minutes to remove the oil, and drain. Rinse with warm water, and then press with both hands to remove the water.

3. Put the mixture A in the pot over medium heat. When it comes to a boil, spread out the abura-age and add it. Put a drop lid in the pot and simmer for about 20 minutes until most of the liquid has evaporated. Spread the abura-age in a strainer and let it drain while cooling. Use both hands to press gently on the abura-age and remove excess liquid. To make it easy to stuff the rice into the abura-age, fold the opening of the abura-age halfway back.

4. Chop the shibazuke pickles and add them to the vinegared rice. Add sesame and mix roughly, then mold lightly into 6 balls.

5. Put the vinegared rice 4 into the abura-age 3. Make sure the rice is fully stuffed into the abura-age, including the corners, and finish by gently patting into shape.

赤飯
FESTIVE RED RICE

お祝いの席に登場する赤飯は、炊飯器で手軽に炊けます。お好みで、ごま塩をかけても。

This red rice, usually served at celebration events, can be easily cooked with a rice cooker.
Serve with sesame and salt, to your liking.

309 kcal
1人分
One serving

材料 (4人分)

もち米 ················· 2合 (360ml)
ささげ ············· ⅓カップ (約67ml)

作り方

1. ささげはなべに入れ、たっぷりの水を注ぎ、中火にかける。煮立ったら2～3分ゆで、ざるに上げて湯を捨てる。ささげを再びなべに入れて水200mlを加え、再び中火にかけて、煮立ったら弱火で15分ゆでる。

2. ①をざるに上げ、豆とゆで汁に分ける。

3. もち米を洗ってざるに上げ、水をきって炊飯器の内がまに入れる。②のゆで汁に水を加えて200mlにし、これを内がまに加える。

4. さらに2合の目盛りまで水を足す。全体をまぜて表面を平らにならし、②の豆を広げてのせ、炊く。

5. 炊き上がったら、さっくりとまぜる。

Ingredients (4 servings)

2cups (360ml) mochi-gome (glutinous rice)
⅓ cup (about 67ml) red beans

Directions

1. Put the beans in a pot, fill with water, and put on medium heat. Allow the beans to boil for 2 or 3 minutes and pour out the water using a strainer. Put the beans back in the pot and add 200 ml of water. Heat at medium heat again and bring to a boil. Simmer at low heat for 15 minutes.

2. Drain the liquid from the beans using a strainer, this time saving the liquid.

3. Wash the glutinous rice and drain out the water with a strainer. Put the rice in a rice cooker. Make a 200ml mixture by adding the bean liquid from 2 and put into the rice cooker.

4. Add water up to the part marked for two cups of rice. Stir the mixture in the rice cooker and level. Spread the beans over the top and cook.

5. When cooked, mix roughly.

おにぎり
ONIGIRI RICE BALLS

具はお好みで用意を。外側はしっかり、中はふんわり握るのがポイント。
Put in the ingredients that you like. The key is to have a firm exterior and an airy interior.

407 kcal
1人分
One serving

材料

熱々のごはん……………………適宜
塩鮭………………………………適宜
甘塩たらこ………………………適宜
梅干し……………………………適宜

作り方

1. 塩鮭は焼いて皮と骨をとり除き、大きくほぐす。たらこは軽く焼いて1cm厚さに切る。梅干しは種をとり除く。ごはんは熱々を用意。手水（水1カップ・200mlに塩小さじ1・5mlの割合でまぜたもの）も用意する。

2. ごはんは、茶わんなどの小さな器に入れてから握る。ごはん量の目安が分かりやすく、おにぎりの大きさがそろう。

3. 両手のひらを手水で軽く濡らし、左手に②のごはんをのせ、まん中にくぼみをつける。手水の塩分でごはんの表面に塩味がつき、くぼみを作ることで具がおにぎりの中心になる。

4. 具をごはんのくぼみにのせる。

5. 具を包みこむようにしてごはんを寄せ、軽くまとめる。

6. 好みの形にととのえながら握る。三角形のおにぎりは、右手の指のつけ根で角を作るようにし、左手の指先と手のひらで軽くごはんをはさんで、手前に転がしながら握る。好みでごまを振りかけたり、焼きのりを貼って仕上げる。

Ingredients

Steaming hot rice, as needed
Salted salmon, as needed
Lightly salted cod roe, as needed
Umeboshi plum, as needed

Directions

1. Cook the salmon and remove the skin and bones. Break it up into large pieces. Lightly cook the cod roe and cut it into 1cm pieces. Remove the seeds from the umeboshi. Ready some steaming hot rice and a mixture of water and salt (5ml of salt to 200ml of water).

2. Before shaping the rice with your hands, put it in a small container, such as a rice bowl. This will make it easy to roughly determine the size, and the rice balls will have a uniform size.

3. Wet both hands in the salt and water solution. Place the rice from 2 on your left hand and make a depression in the middle. The outer part of the rice will acquire a salty taste from the salt and water solution, and the ingredients will be at the center of the onigiri where the depression is.

4. Put the ingredients inside the depression.

5. Gently close the opening with rice so that the ingredients are covered in rice on all sides.

6. Squeeze the onigiri into the desired shape. For a triangular onigiri, make the corners with the lower part of your right hand fingers, using your left finger tips and palm to lightly pat the onigiri as you turn it toward yourself. You can add sesame and cover the onigiri with roasted nori seaweed if you like.

きのこの炊き込みごはん
RICE COOKED WITH MUSHROOMS

具と米をかきまぜると炊きむらができることがあるので、具はそっとのせるだけ。
Stirring the ingredients and rice will leave some parts uncooked. Just put the ingredients on top of the rice.

483 kcal
1人分
One serving

材料（2〜3人分）

米	………………………	2合(360ml)
生しいたけ	…………………	1パック
しめじ	………………………	1パック
にんじん	……………………	小½本
鶏胸肉	…………………	½枚(100g)

A
酒	…………………	小さじ1(5ml)
しょうゆ	…………	小さじ1(5ml)

B
酒	……………	大さじ1 (15ml)
塩	…………	小さじ¾ (3.75ml)
しょうゆ	…………	小さじ2(10ml)
みりん	…………	小さじ2(10ml)

🔍 作る前にしておくこと

米は炊く30分前にといで、
ざるに上げておく。

Preparations

Wash the rice 30 minutes before
you begin to cook it, and let it
sit in a strainer.

作り方

1. しいたけ、しめじは石づきを切り、し
いたけは薄切り、しめじはほぐす。
にんじんは7〜8mm角に切る。

2. 鶏肉は小さめのそぎ切りにし、Aの
酒、しょうゆをからめて下味をつける。

3. 炊飯器に米を入れ、水をひたひた
に注いでBの酒、塩、しょうゆ、み
りんを入れて調味する。

4. 目盛りまで水を足して普通に水かげ
んし、ひとまぜして表面を平にする。

5. しめじ、しいたけ、鶏肉、にんじん
を広げてのせ、普通に炊く。

6. 炊き上がったらさっくりとまぜて、器
に盛る。

Ingredients (2-3 servings)

2 cups (360ml) rice
1 pack raw shiitake mushrooms
1 pack shimeji mushrooms
½ small carrot
½ piece (100g) chicken breast

A | 1 tsp (5ml) sake
  | 1 tsp (5ml) soy sauce

B | 1 tbsp (15ml) sake
  | ¾ tsp (3.75ml) salt
  | 2 tsp (10ml) soy sauce
  | 2 tsp (10ml) mirin (sweet sake)

Directions

1. Cut off the hard ends from the mushrooms,
and thinly slice the shiitake and break the
shimeji into pieces. Cut the carrot into
7 or 8mm pieces.

2. Slice the chicken by making small, thin
diagonal cuts, and put into sake and soy
sauce A to marinate.

3. Put rice in a rice cooker, pour in water so it
barely covers the rice, and put in sake, salt,
soy sauce and mirin B for flavoring.

4. Add water to the normal level using the
scale on the rice cooker. Stir a little and
flatten the surface of the rice.

5. Spread out shimeji and shiitake mushrooms, chicken, and carrots on the rice and
cook as usual.

6. When it's finished cooking, roughly stir and
scoop into a serving dish.

← 具をのせたらかきまぜないで炊く
Cook the rice without stirring
in the added ingredients.

かやくごはん

KAYAKU MIXED RICE

野菜を切るときは大きさをそろえて。これもおいしさのための大切なポイントの一つです。
Cut all vegetables to the same length. This will also make for delicious results.

456 kcal

1人分
One serving

材料 (2～3人分)

米 …………………… 2合 (360ml)
にんじん …………………… 小1本
ごぼう …………………… 大½本
油揚げ …………………… 1枚

A | 酒 …………… 大さじ1 (15ml)
　 | 塩 ………… 小さじ¾ (3.75ml)
　 | しょうゆ ……… 大さじ1 (15ml)

青のり …………………… 少々

♪ 作る前にしておくこと

米は炊く30分前にといで、
ざるに上げておく。

Preparations

Wash the rice 30 minutes before
you begin to cook it, and let it
sit in a strainer.

作り方

1. にんじんはせん切り、ごぼうは皮をこ
　そげてささがきにし、水にさらす。油
　揚げは油抜きして細切りにする。

2. 炊飯器に米を入れて目盛りまで水を
　入れる。大さじ3 (45ml)の水をすく
　い出し、Aを加えてひとまぜする。

3. 表面を平らにして水けをきった具を
　広げてのせ、普通に炊く。さっくりと
　まぜて器に盛り、青のりを振る。

Ingredients (2-3 servings)

2 cups (360ml) rice
1 small carrot
½ large burdock
1 slice abura-age (deep-fried tofu)

A | 1 tbsp (15ml) sake
　 | ¾ tsp (3.75ml) salt
　 | 1 tbsp (15ml) soy sauce

Ao-nori green laver flakes, to your taste

← 切り方や大きさをそろえる
Cut ingredients the same way
and in consistent sizes.

Directions

1. Julienne the carrots, scrape the skin off the
   burdock root and cut it into matchstick-
   size pieces by shaving it from the outside,
   then soak them in water. Remove the oil
   from the abura-age by pouring hot water
   over it, and cut it into strips.

2. Add the rice and water to the appropriate
   level on the scale. Remove 3 tbsp (45ml) of
   the water and lightly mix in A.

3. Flatten the surface, then spread out the
   drained ingredients on top. Cook as usual.
   Stir roughly, put in a serving dish and
   sprinkle on the ao-nori green laver flakes.

和風カレーライス

JAPANESE CURRY RICE

懐かしい香りのカレー。昔からどこの家庭でも作られているおふくろの味です。
Try this nostalgic and aromatic curry.
It is a homemade flavor that Japanese mothers have made for their families for a long time.

983 kcal
1人分
One serving

材料（2人分）

ごはん	2皿分
豚ロース薄切り肉	200g
じゃがいも	大1個（200g）
玉ねぎ	1個
にんじん	1本
トマト	大1個
にんにくのみじん切り	1かけ分
しょうがのみじん切り	1かけ分
赤とうがらしの小口切り	1本分

A
塩	小さじ⅓（約1.7ml）
こしょう	少々
カレー粉	小さじ1（5ml）

カレー粉	大さじ1（15ml）
サラダ油	大さじ1（15ml）
小麦粉	大さじ1.5（22.5ml）

B
だし	大さじ2（30ml）
しょうゆ	大さじ1.5（22.5ml）
みりん	大さじ1（15ml）

福神漬、らっきょうなど好みの薬味
 …………………………… 適宜

作り方

1. 豚肉は食べやすく切る。Aの塩、こしょう、カレー粉を振り、よくもみ込んで下味をつける。

2. じゃがいもは一口大に切り、水にさらして水けをきる。玉ねぎはくし形切り、にんじんは乱切りにする。

3. サラダ油を熱し、にんにく、しょうが、赤とうがらしを炒め、香りが立ったらカレー粉を入れて炒める。

4. 豚肉を加えて炒め、肉の色が変わったら、じゃがいも、玉ねぎ、にんじんを加えて炒め合わせる。

5. 油が回ったら、小麦粉を振り入れてさらに炒める。

6. ざく切りにしたトマト、Bを加えてよくまぜ、とろりとするまで15〜20分煮込む。ごはんにかけて食べる。

Ingredients (2 servings)

2 servings cooked rice
200g thinly sliced loin pork meat
1 (200g) large potato
1 onion
1 carrot
1 large tomato
1 clove chopped garlic
1 clove chopped ginger
1 finely cut red hot pepper

A | ⅓ tsp (about 1.7ml) salt
  | Pepper, to your taste
  | 1 tsp (5ml) curry powder

1 tbsp (15ml) curry powder
1 tbsp (15ml) salad oil
1.5 tbsp (22.5ml) flour

B | 2 tbsp (30ml) soup stock
  | 1.5 tbsp (22.5ml) soy sauce
  | 1 tbsp (15ml) mirin (sweet sake)

Fukujinzuke pickles, shallots or other condiments, as needed

Directions

1. Cut the pork into easy-to-eat pieces. Sprinkle on the salt, pepper and curry powder A, and then knead it into the meat.

2. Cut the potato into bite-size pieces, rinse with water and drain. Cut the onion into wedges and the carrot into chunks.

3. Heat the oil and fry the garlic, ginger and red pepper. When the aroma comes out, add the curry powder and fry.

4. Add the pork and fry. When the meat changes color, add the potatoes, onions and carrots, and stir-fry together.

5. When the oil is dispersed, sprinkle on the flour and fry some more.

6. Add a roughly cut tomato and B and stir well. Let it simmer for 15 to 20 minutes until the curry thickens. Scoop some curry on top of rice and enjoy!

親子丼

OYAKO-DON (CHICKEN AND EGG ON RICE)

卵は半熟状にふっくら火を通すのがポイントです。
The main thing is to poach the egg so it is soft boiled.

619 kcal
1人分
One serving

Ingredients (2 servings)

2 donburi bowls cooked rice
½ chicken breast
2 eggs
½ onion

A | ¾ cup (150ml) soup stock
  | 1 tbsp (15ml) mirin (sweet sake)
  | 1 tbsp (15ml) soy sauce

Roasted nori seaweed sheets, as needed

Directions

1. Slice the chicken diagonally into bite-size pieces, and cut the onion into wedges.

2. Put in A, heat to a boil, then add the chicken. Bring to a boil again and add the onions. Let it boil for 4 to 5 minutes. Stir in the beaten egg.

3. Cover immediately with a lid and turn the heat to low. Steam for 30 seconds and then turn off the heat. Dish onto the rice and sprinkle little pieces of nori seaweed on top.

材料（2人分）

ごはん ……………… どんぶり2杯分
鶏胸肉 ………………………… ½枚
卵 ……………………………… 2個
玉ねぎ ………………………… ½個

A | だし ……… ¾カップ（150ml）
  | みりん ……… 大さじ1（15ml）
  | しょうゆ …… 大さじ1（15ml）

焼きのり ……………………… 適宜

作り方

1. 鶏肉は一口大のそぎ切りにし、玉ねぎはくし形切りにする。

2. Aを合わせ、煮立ったら鶏肉を入れる。再び煮立ったら玉ねぎを加えて4〜5分煮、とき卵を回し入れる。

3. すぐふたをして弱火にし、30秒ほど蒸らして火を止める。ごはんに具をのせて、ちぎったのりを散らす。

とき卵は煮立っているところに
Add the egg just when the ingredients start to bubble up...

牛丼
BEEF-DON (BEEF ON RICE)

三つ葉が香りのアクセント。
With the fragrant accent of the mitsuba trefoil.

617 kcal
1人分
One serving

Ingredients (2 servings)

2 donburi bowls cooked rice
100g beef sliced into small strips
½ onion

A | ⅔ cup (about 134ml) soup stock
  | 2 tbsp (30ml) soy sauce
  | 2 tbsp (30ml) mirin (sweet sake)

½ bunch mitsuba trefoil

Directions

1. Cut the onion in half vertically. Peel off about two onion layers at a time and cut them into wedges from the edge.

2. Mix the soup stock, soy sauce, and mirin in A together, and bring to a boil. Add onions and beef, in that order, and remove the scum.

3. Simmer for 3 or 4 minutes, then add the mitsuba trefoil cut to a length of 3 cm, and bring to a boil. Place the ingredients on a bowl of rice.

肉は玉ねぎにさっと火が通ったら入れます

Put the onions in first and lightly cook, Then put in the meat.

材料（2人分）

ごはん……………どんぶり2杯分
牛こまぎれ肉………………100g
玉ねぎ………………………½個

A | だし……⅔カップ（約134ml）
  | しょうゆ………大さじ2（30ml）
  | みりん………大さじ2（30ml）

三つ葉…………………………½束

作り方

1. 縦半分にした玉ねぎは2枚ずつくらいにはがして、端からくし形に切る。

2. Aのだし、しょうゆ、みりんを合わせ、煮立ったら玉ねぎ、牛肉の順に入れてアクをとる。

3. 3〜4分煮て火を通し、3cm長さに切った三つ葉を加えて一煮する。ごはんに具をのせる。

そぼろ丼

SOBORO ON RICE

コクのある豚ひき肉のそぼろといり卵をのせて。
Put soboro (full-flavored ground pork) and scrambled eggs on your rice.

634 kcal
1人分
One serving

材料（2人分）

ごはん ················· どんぶり2杯分
豚ひき肉 ······························100g
卵 ···2個

A | 塩 ·······································少々
　 | 砂糖 ·············· 大さじ½ (7.5ml)

B | 酒 ················· 小さじ1 (5ml)
　 | 砂糖 ············· 小さじ1 (5ml)
　 | しょうゆ ········· 小さじ2 (10ml)

三つ葉 ·································½束
しょうゆ ················ 小さじ1 (5ml)

作り方

1. とき卵にAをまぜてフライパンに入れ、火にかける。菜箸4本でポロポロになるまで手早くまぜて火を通す。

2. フライパンにひき肉とBを入れ、よくまぜて火にかける。菜箸4本でポロポロになるまでまぜて火を通す。

3. 三つ葉をさっとゆでて刻み、水けをしぼってしょうゆをからめる。ごはんに①、②をのせ、三つ葉をあしらう。

Ingredients (2 servings)

2 donburi bowls cooked rice
100g ground pork
2 eggs

A | Salt, to your taste
　 | ½ tbsp (7.5ml) sugar

B | 1 tsp (5ml) sake
　 | 1 tsp (5ml) sugar
　 | 2 tsp (10ml) soy sauce

½ bunch mitsuba trefoil
1 tsp (5ml) soy sauce

Directions

1. Mix A into the beaten eggs and heat in a frying pan. Cook quickly with 4 large chopsticks until the mix is well scrambled and heated through.

2. Put the meat and B in a frying pan and heat while mixing. Cook with 4 large chopsticks until the mix is well scrambled and heated through.

3. Blanch and chop the mitsuba trefoil, squeeze out the water and mix with soy sauce. Spread 1 and 2 on top of the rice, then finish with the mitsuba trefoil.

火を通す前に肉と調味料をまぜる
Mix the meat and seasonings before heating through.

おろしそば

OROSHI SOBA NOODLES

大根おろし、蒸し鶏、わかめ、梅肉を添えてさっぱりと。
Grated daikon radish, steamed chicken, wakame seaweed and umeboshi meat make for a refreshing meal.

389 kcal

1人分
One serving

材料（2人分）

干しそば ……………………… 150g
大根 ……………………………… 150g
カットわかめ（乾燥）…………… 2g
鶏ささ身 ……………………………2本
梅干し ……………………………1個

A｜だし ………… 1.5カップ（300ml）
　｜砂糖 ……………… 小さじ1（5ml）
　｜しょうゆ ………… 大さじ2（30ml）
　｜みりん …………… 大さじ2（30ml）

B｜塩 ……………………………… 少々
　｜酒 ………………… 大さじ1（15ml）

ねりわさび ………………………… 少々

作り方

1. Aを合わせ、一煮立ちさせてつゆを作り、冷やしておく。

2. 大根はおろしてざるに上げ、水けをきる。わかめは水でもどし、水けをよくしぼる。

3. 小なべにささ身を入れ、Bを振り入れて下味をつける。湯¼カップ（50ml）を加えて蒸し煮にし、そのまま冷まして細く裂く。

4. そばはそうめん（p.53）と同様にゆで、もみ洗いしてざるに上げ、水けをきる。

5. 器に盛り、わかめ、ささ身、ちぎった梅干し、大根おろし、わさびをのせて、つゆを張る。

Ingredients (2 servings)

150g dried soba
150g daikon radish
2g cut wakame seaweed (dried)
2 chicken fillets
1 umeboshi plum

A｜1.5 cups (300ml) soup stock
　｜1 tsp (5ml) sugar
　｜2 tbsp (30ml) soy sauce
　｜2 tbsp (30ml) mirin (sweet sake)

B｜Salt, to your taste
　｜1 tbsp (15ml) sake

Wasabi paste, to your taste

Directions

1. Mix all A ingredients, bring to a boil to make a noodle dipping sauce, then cool.

2. Place the grated daikon radish in a strainer to drain the moisture. Soak the wakame seaweed in water to soften it, and then firmly squeeze out the water.

3. Steam the seasoned chicken with B in a small pot with ¼ cup (50ml) of hot water. Take the chicken out after steaming and leave it for a while to cool. Then, tear it into narrow strips.

4. Boil the soba the same way as somen noodles (see page 53). Rinse by hand in water, and then place in a strainer to drain the water.

5. Place noodles in a dish, then top with wakame seaweed, the chicken fillets, umeboshi meat, grated daikon radish, and wasabi, and finally pour in the noodle dipping sause.

下味をつけたささ身に湯を加えてふたをし、7〜8分蒸し煮にして火を通します。うまみを逃がさないように、ふたをしたまま冷ましてから細く裂きます。

Use a lid when steaming the seasoned chicken fillets and heat through for 7 to 8 minutes. Cool with the lid on the pan so that the umami flavor doesn't escape from the chicken, then tear it into narrow strips.

五目そうめん

GOMOKU SOMEN (WITH ASSORTED INGREDIENTS)

そうめんは具を彩りよくのせて、食べる直前につゆを張ります。
Add colorful assorted ingredients, and put noodle sauce just before sarving.

463 kcal
1人分
One serving

材料（2人分）

そうめん ……………………… 150g
うなぎのかば焼き ……………… ½尾
卵焼き …………………………… 1個分
トマト …………………………… ½個
きゅうり ………………………… ½本
グリーンアスパラガス ………… 4本

A｜だし ………… 1.5 カップ（300ml）
　｜しょうゆ ………… 大さじ1（15ml）
　｜みりん …………… 大さじ2（30ml）
　｜塩 …………… 小さじ¼（1.25ml）

いり白ごま ……………………… 少々

作り方

1. Aを合わせ、一煮立ちさせてつゆを作り、冷やしておく。

2. そうめんはゆでる。

3. うなぎ、卵焼き、トマトは食べやすく切り、きゅうりは小口切りにする。アスパラはこんがり焼いて4cm長さに切る。

4. 器にそうめんを盛り、③をのせてごまを振り、つゆを張る。

Ingredients (2 servings)

150g somen noodles
½ broiled eel
1 rolled egg omelet
½ tomato
½ cucumber
4 green asparagus stalks

A｜1.5 cups (300ml) soup stock
　｜1 tbsp (15ml) soy sauce
　｜2 tbsp (30ml) mirin (sweet-sake)
　｜¼ tsp (1.25ml) salt

Roasted white sesame, to your taste

Directions

1. Mix all the ingredients in A and heat to a boil to make the soup sauce, then allow to cool.

2. Boil the somen noodles.

3. Cut the eel, rolled egg, and tomato into bite-size pieces and cut the cucumber into small thin pieces. Roast the asparagus and cut into 4cm lengths.

4. Arrange the somen noodles in a dish, add the ingredients in 3, sprinkle on sesame and serve with noodle sauce.

そうめんのゆで方

1. なべにたっぷりの湯を沸かし、そうめんをさばきながらパラパラと手早く入れ、菜箸で大きくかきまぜる。

2. 沸騰したらさし水をする。再び煮立ったら、めんを1本水にとって食べ、ゆでかげんをみる。

3. 湯をきって流水で軽くもみ洗いし、ざるに上げて水けをよくきる。

How to boil somen noodles

1. Bring a pot full of water to a boil, then quickly slip in the noodles, while stirring robustly with large chopsticks.

2. When it starts to boil over, add water. When it boils again, take one noodle and bite it to check the doneness.

3. Drain the boiling water, rinse by hand in running water and place on a strainer to drain the water.

煮込みうどん
UDON STEW

はりはりとした水菜の歯ざわりが絶妙。鶏肉からもだしが出てコクもじゅうぶんの、あたたまる一品。
Fresh mizuna greens go well with the dish and give it a crisp texture, creating a comfort food with plenty of rich stock from chicken. Serve as a warming treat for the body and soul.

495 kcal
1人分
One serving

材料（2人分）

うどん（冷凍）‥‥‥‥‥‥‥‥ 2玉
鶏もも肉‥‥‥‥‥‥‥‥‥1枚 (200g)
水菜‥‥‥‥‥‥‥‥‥‥‥‥ 200g

A｜だし‥‥‥‥‥ 3.5カップ (700ml)
　｜酒‥‥‥‥‥‥‥‥ 大さじ2 (30ml)
　｜塩‥‥‥‥‥‥‥ 小さじ½ (2.5ml)
　｜みりん‥‥‥‥‥‥大さじ1 (15ml)
　｜しょうゆ‥‥‥‥‥大さじ½ (7.5ml)

作り方

1. 鶏肉は一口大に切り、水菜は5〜6cm長さに切る。

2. Aを合わせて火にかけ、煮立ったら鶏肉を入れて7〜8分煮る。

3. うどんを凍ったまま入れて、さらに煮込む。

4. 水菜を加えて一煮する。

Ingredients (2 servings)

2 packs udon noodles (frozen)
1 (200g) chicken thigh
200g mizuna greens

A｜3.5 cups (700ml) soup stock
　｜2 tbsp (30ml) sake
　｜½ tsp (2.5ml) salt
　｜1 tbsp (15ml) mirin (sweet sake)
　｜½ tbsp (7.5ml) soy sauce

Directions

1. Cut the chicken into bite-size pieces. Cut the mizuna greens into lengths of 5 to 6 cm.

2. Mix all the ingredients in A and heat. Bring to a boil, and put in the chicken, then boil for 7 to 8 minutes.

3. Put in the frozen udon noodles and leave it to boil.

4. Add the mizuna greens, and bring to a boil, then turn off the heat.

POINTER

冷凍うどんは凍ったまま煮立った煮汁に入れ、自然にほぐれてきたら菜箸でほぐします。ゆでめんを使う場合は、熱湯にさっとくぐらせてぬめりをとってから煮込みます。

When you put the frozen udon noodles in the boiling soup, stir with large chopsticks only after the udon has naturally started to separate. If you are using boiled noodles, first pour boiling water over them to get rid of the excess starch and then put them into the boiling soup.

🔍 クッキングメモ

うどんは目的と好みに合わせて

うどんは目的の料理に合った太さを選ぶことが大切です。ここでは冷凍うどんを使っていますが、乾めん、生めん、ゆでめんなど、お好みでどうぞ。乾めんを使う場合は袋の表示を目安に、少しかためにゆで上げて、手早く水にさらし、もみ洗いしてぬめりをとり、水けをよくきってから煮込みます。生めんを使う場合は、ゆでる前に打ち粉をはたき落としてからさばき入れます。

🔍 COOKING MEMO

Use udon noodles to match the specific dish and preference.

It is important to choose the thickness of the udon noodles to match the dish. Here we are using frozen noodles, but you may use dried noodles, fresh noodles or boiled noodles. If you are using dried noodles, follow the instructions on the package and take it out when still a little firm, rinse with water to remove the sliminess, drain, then simmer in the soup. If you are using fresh noodles, dust off the excess flour before boiling.

すき焼き
SUKIYAKI

関東風にわりしたで味つけ。わりしたは一度に入れすぎないで、そのつど補うのがおいしさの秘訣。
Cook the meat and add the kanto-style sukiyaki broth.
The secret is not to add too much at one time and to control the good taste.

670 kcal
1人分
One serving

材料（2人分）

牛ロース肉（すき焼き用）………300g
しらたき ………………………1袋
焼き豆腐 ………………………1丁
ねぎ ……………………………2本
春菊 ……………………………1束
卵 ………………………………適宜

A｜しょうゆ ……… ¾カップ（150ml）
　｜砂糖 …………… 大さじ2（30ml）
　｜水 ……………… 1カップ（200ml）
　｜みりん…………½カップ（100ml）

牛脂 ……………………………適宜

作り方

1. 小なべにAのしょうゆ、砂糖、水、みりんを合わせて一煮立ちさせ、わりしたを作る。

2. しらたきはざっと刻んで、煮立った湯に入れて1〜2分煮立て、ざるに上げて湯をきる。

3. 豆腐は一口大に切る。ねぎは斜め切りにし、春菊は葉先をつんでおく。

4. すき焼きなべをよく熱し、牛脂を焼いて脂を出す。牛肉を入れてさっと両面を焼きつける。

5. ねぎを加えてわりしたを注ぐ。しらたき、焼き豆腐、春菊を加え、煮えた順にとき卵にくぐらせて食べる。

Ingredients (2 servings)

300g sliced beef loin (cut for sukiyaki)
1 bag shirataki
1 block grilled tofu
2 naganegi onions
1 garland chrysanthemum stalk
Egg, as needed

A｜¾ cup (150ml) soy sauce
　｜2 tbsp (30ml) sugar
　｜1 cup (200ml) water
　｜½ cup (100ml) mirin (sweet sake)

Beef tallow, as needed

← 熱湯でゆでて石灰のくさみをとる
Remove the lime taste by boiling it in hot water.

Directions

1. Make the broth. Put the soy sauce, sugar, water and mirin from A into a small pot and let it come to a boil.

2. Cut up the shirataki roughly and put it in boiling water for 1 to 2 minutes, then place in a strainer to drain the hot water.

3. Cut the tofu into bite-size pieces. Cut the naganegi onions at an angle, and cut off the tips of the garland chrysanthemum.

4. Heat the sukiyaki pot well to cook out the beef tallow. Quickly cook the beef on both sides.

5. Add the naganegi onions and pour the broth. Then add the shirataki, grilled tofu, and the garland chrysanthemum. Pick bite-size portions from the pot as the ingredients cook. You can dip them in beaten raw egg if you like.

なべ・汁もの
Hot Soup

おでん
ODEN

だしが決め手の関東炊きです。
Soup stock gives kanto-style oden its distinctive taste.

304 kcal
1人分
One serving

材料 (4人分)

◎具

大根	½本
こぶ (3×30cm 角)	4枚
こんにゃく	1枚
がんもどき	4個
厚揚げ	1枚
卵	4個
ちくわぶ	1本
ちくわ	4本
ごぼう巻きや魚ボールなど 好みのねり製品	適宜

◎つゆ

だし (こぶと削りがつおで)	6カップ (1200ml)
酒	½カップ (100ml)
みりん	大さじ3 (45ml)
しょうゆ	大さじ2 (30ml)
塩	小さじ1 (5ml)

◎薬味

ねりがらし	適宜

作り方

1. P24を参考にしてこぶと削りがつおでだしをとる。

2. がんもどき、厚揚げ、ねり製品はひとゆでして油抜きをする。

3. こぶは水でもどし、結び目を作って切る。

4. 卵はゆでて殻をむく。

5. 大根は皮をむいて2～3cm厚さの輪切りにする。こんにゃくは表面にこまかい格子状の切り込みを入れて4等分に切り、下ゆでしてアクを抜く。厚揚げは4等分に切る。ちくわぶは3～4cm厚さの斜め切りにする。

6. なべにつゆの材料と大根、こぶ、こんにゃくを入れて火にかけ、煮立ったら弱火にして30～40分煮る。大根がやわらかくなったら、がんもどき、厚揚げ、ゆで卵を加えて20分、残りの材料を加えてさらに15～20分煮て味をしみ込ませる。器にとり分け、からしをつけて食べる。

Ingredients (4 servings)

◎ Main ingredients

½ daikon radish
4 (3 × 30cm) pieces kobu seaweed
1 block konnyaku
4 balls ganmodoki (deep-fried tofu mixed with thinly sliced vegetables)
1 block atsu-age (deep-fried tofu)
4 eggs
1 chikuwabu roll
4 chikuwa rolls
Gobo-maki, fish balls, and other fish-paste based items, as needed

◎ Soup broth

6 cups (1200ml) soup stock
½ cup (100ml) sake
3 tbsp (45ml) mirin (sweet sake)
2 tbsp (30ml) soy sauce
1 tsp (5ml) salt

◎ Condiments

Karashi paste (Japanese mustard), as needed

Directions

1. With page 24 as a reference, use kobu seaweed and dried bonito to make the soup stock.

2. Boil the ganmodoki, atsu-age, and other deep-fried fish-paste items, and then remove the oil by rinsing with hot water.

3. Soften the kobu with water and tie knots, then cut.

4. Boil the eggs and peel.

5. Peel the daikon radish and cut it into round pieces 2 to 3 cm thick. Cut cross sections, like a thin grid, on the surface of the konnyaku, and cut into 4 equal parts, then boil and remove the scum. Cut the atsu-age into 4 equal parts. Diagonally cut the chikuwabu into 3 or 4 cm thick pieces.

6. Put the soup broth ingredients into a pot, and add the daikon radish, kobu, konnyaku and heat. When it comes to a boil, turn the heat to low and let it simmer for 30 to 40 minutes. When the daikon radish is soft, add the ganmodoki, atsu-age and hard-boiled eggs and simmer for 20 minutes. Then add the rest of the ingredients and simmer for 15 to 20 minutes to braise them. Serve with a little karashi on the side.

POINTER!

がんもどきや厚揚げなど油で揚げてあるものは、さっとゆでて油抜きすると、おいしく仕上がる。

Slightly boiling the fried ingredients, such as ganmodoki and atsu-age, will remove the oil and make them taste better.

しっかりとだしをしみ込ませるには、材料を煮る順番がたいせつ。

It's important to follow the correct order when boiling the ingredients to ensure that the flavor of the stock seeps in well.

しゃぶしゃぶ
SHABU SHABU

つけだれを手作りするとおいしい。
It's delicious if you make your own dipping sauce.

325 kcal
1人分
One serving

材料（4人分）

◎具
牛肉 (しゃぶしゃぶ用)・・・・・・・・・400g
にんじん・・・・・・・・・・・・・・・・・・・・・・・1本
ねぎ・・・・・・・・・・・・・・・・・・・・・・・・・・・2本
にら・・・・・・・・・・・・・・・・・・・・・・・・・・・1束

◎つゆ
酒・・・・・・・・・・・・・・・・・¼カップ (50ml)
水・・・・・・・・・・・・・・・・・・・・・・・・・・・・適宜

◎つけだれ（ポン酢じょうゆ）
ポン酢じょうゆ・・・・・・・・・・・・・・・・適宜

◎つけだれ（ごまだれ）
だし・・・・・・・・・・・・・・・・・大さじ6 (90ml)
ねりごま・・・・・・・・・・・・・大さじ4 (60ml)
しょうゆ、砂糖、酢・・・各大さじ1(15ml)

◎薬味
万能ねぎの小口切り、おろししょうが、
一味とうがらし・・・・・・・・・・・・・各適宜

作り方

1. 肉は一枚一枚ていねいに広げ、箸でとりやすいように器に盛る。

2. にんじんはピーラーで10cm長さにスライスする。ねぎは10cm長さに切り、切り込みを入れて芯をとり除き、1cm幅に縦に切る。にらは10cm長さに切る。

3. ごまだれの材料をまぜる。

4. なべに酒を入れて水を七分目まで注ぐ。

5. ④を火にかけ、煮立ったら①と②を食べる分ずつ入れ、火が通ったものから好みのつけだれと薬味で食べる。

Ingredients (4 servings)

◎ Main ingredients
400g beef (sliced for shabu shabu)
1 carrot
2 naganegi onions
1 bunch garlic chives

◎ Soup broth
¼ cup (50ml) sake
Water, as needed

◎ Dipping sauce (ponzu)
Ponzu, as needed

◎ Dipping sauce (sesame sauce)
6 tbsp (90ml) soup stock
4 tbsp (60ml) sesame paste
1 tbsp (15ml) each soy sauce, sugar, vinegar

◎ Condiments
Banno-negi onions cut into thin pieces,
grated ginger and ichimi spice, as needed

Directions

1. Carefully spread out and display each slice of beef so it can be easily picked up with chopsticks.

2. Slice the carrot with a peeler to 10cm long slices. Cut the naganegi onions into lengths of 10 cm, cut out the core and cut the outer part into 1cm widths lengthwise. Cut the garlic chives in to 10cm lengths.

3. Mix together all the ingredients in the sesame sauce.

4. Put the sake into the pot and fill the pot up to 70% with water.

5. Heat 4. When it starts to boil. Add portion of 1 and 2. When the ingredients are heated through, begin eating your favorites with the dipping sauces and condiments.

なべ・汁もの
Hot Soup

POINTER!

牛肉はごく薄切りのものを。さっぱりとした肉が好きな人は、もも肉など脂身の少ない肉を選んで。

Buy beef that is cut especially thin for use in shabu shabu. If you prefer meat with a light texture, select thinly sliced beef with little fat.

🔍 中国から伝わった しゃぶしゃぶ

しゃぶしゃぶは、涮羊肉（サンヤンロウ）という羊肉を使ったなべ料理が中国から伝わったのが起源とされ、日本人に抵抗のない牛肉でアレンジされ、現在のように広まったようです。
　煮立った湯の中で肉をしゃぶしゃぶと泳がすことからこの名がつきました。

🔍 Shabu shabu was passed down from China

The shabu shabu hot pot was introduced from China. Originally, it was made with san-yan-rou(lamb or mutton), but the Japanese used beef, which they were more familiar with. That is how it is most often prepared throughout Japan now.

The origin of the name comes from the sound made when the meat is dipped into the boiling water.

湯豆腐
BOILED TOFU

豆腐の滋味を味わいたい冬の定番なべ。
A common winter dish to enjoy the flavor of tofu.

156 kcal
1人分
One serving

材料 (4人分)

◎具
木綿豆腐 ……………………… 2丁
ねぎ ……………………………… 3本

◎つゆ
こぶ (10cm角) ………………… 1枚
水 ………………………………… 適宜

◎つけだれ (土佐じょうゆ)
削りがつお ……………………… 5g
しょうゆ ………… ½カップ (100ml)
酒 ………………… 大さじ2 (30ml)

◎薬味
あさつきの小口切り、
　半すり白ごま、すだち ……… 各適宜

作り方

1. 土なべにこぶを入れて水を七分目ぐ
   らいまで注ぎ、20分ほどおく。

2. 豆腐はやっこに切り、ねぎは斜め切
   りにする。

3. 小なべにしょうゆと酒を入れて煮立
   て、削りがつおを加えて一煮し、火
   を止めて万能こし器などでこし、土
   佐じょうゆを作る。

4. ①に豆腐を入れ、中火にかける。
   煮立ったらねぎを加える。煮えたも
   のから土佐じょうゆと好みの薬味で
   食べる。

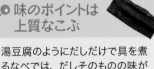

味のポイントは 上質なこぶ

湯豆腐のようにだしだけで具を煮
るなべでは、だしそのものの味が
おいしさを左右します。おいしいこ
ぶだし作りにはこぶ選びが肝心。
品質のよいものは、色が黒くて身
が厚く、よく乾燥したものです。品
質を保つためにはしけないようにし
ます。

Ingredients (4 servings)

◎ Main ingredients
2 packs firm tofu
3 naganegi onions

◎ Soup stock
1 piece kobu seaweed (10 × 10cm)
Water, as needed

◎ Dipping sauce (Tosa soy sauce)
5g shaved dried bonito
½ cup (100ml) soy sauce
2 tbsp (30ml) sake

◎ Condiments
Chopped chives, semi-ground white
sesame, sudachi citrus, as needed

Directions

1. Place the kobu seaweed in an earthen
   pot, and fill up to 70% with water,
   then allow to sit for about 20 minutes.

2. Cut the tofu into 6 or 8 cubes, and cut
   the naganegi onions diagonally.

3. To make the Tosa soy sauce, heat soy
   sauce and sake in a small pot to a
   boil, add the shaved dried bonito and
   cook, then stop heating and strain in
   a strainer.

4. Put the tofu into 1 and heat on
   medium heat. When it comes to a boil,
   add the naganegi onions. Take the
   cooked ingredients and use the Tosa
   soy sauce and any other condiments
   to garnish.

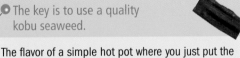

The key is to use a quality kobu seaweed.

The flavor of a simple hot pot where you just put the
main ingredients into the soup stock and cook is
determined by the quality of the soup stock. To make
a delicious kobu soup stock, choosing the kobu is
essential. A good quality kobu is one that has a
black color, is thick, and is dried well. To maintain the
quality of the kobu and keep mildew away.

POINTER!

削りがつおをさっと煮ることで、
しょうゆにかつおのうまみが加
わる。

By briefly boiling the dried
bonito, the flavor of the bonito
will soak into the soy sauce.

寄せなべ
YOSENABE (A HOT POT WITH A LIGHTLY FLAVORED SOUP BROTH)

つゆに薄味がついているので、つゆごといただきます。
You can drink the soup too because it's lightly flavored.

356 kcal
1人分
One serving

64

材料 (4人分)

◎具
鶏胸肉	1枚
きんめだい	2切れ
えび	8尾
白菜	¼株
ねぎ	2本
しめじ	1パック
にんじん	1本(100g)
大根	300g

◎つゆ
酒	¼カップ (50ml)
みりん	大さじ2 (30ml)
しょうゆ	大さじ1 (15ml)
塩	小さじ½ (2.5ml)
だし	4カップ (800ml)

作り方

1. 鶏肉は一口大のそぎ切りにする。きんめだいは一口大に切り、えびは背わたをとる。

2. 白菜は軸と葉に分けてそれぞれ一口大に切り、ねぎは斜め切りにする。しめじは石づきを切り落としてほぐす。にんじん、大根は皮をむいて5mm厚さの輪切りにし、あれば菊型で抜く。

3. 土なべにつゆの材料をすべて入れて中火にかけ、煮立ったら大根とにんじんを入れる。

4. 大根とにんじんに火が通ったら①を加え、残りの野菜やしめじも加えて、煮えたものから食べる。

🔎 つゆに薄味のついた寄せなべ

調理場で残りものを煮て食べたのが始まりといわれる寄せなべは具に決まりがないのが魅力。肉や魚貝類、野菜、豆腐などを自由にアレンジして楽しみましょう。

🔎 Yosenabe hot pot with a lightly flavored soup broth

The yosenabe hot pot, which started off as a dish for cooking leftovers, has no specific ingredients, which is the beauty of this dish. You can put in meat, fish, seafood, vegetables, tofu... anything you think you might enjoy.

Ingredients (4 servings)

◎ Main ingredients
- 1 chicken breast fillet
- 2 kinmedai (alfonsino fish) fillets
- 8 shrimps
- ¼ Napa Chinese cabbage
- 2 naganegi onions
- 1 pack shimeji mushrooms
- 1 carrot (100g)
- 300g daikon radish

◎ Soup broth
- ¼ cup (50ml) sake
- 2 tbsp (30ml) mirin (sweet sake)
- 1 tbsp (15ml) soy sauce
- ½ tsp (2.5ml) salt
- 4 cups (800ml) soup stock

Directions

1. Cut the chicken into bite-size pieces. Cut the kinmedai into bite-size pieces, and de-vein the shrimp.

2. Separate the core and leaves of the Napa Chinese cabbage, and cut it into bite-size pieces. Cut the naganegi onions diagonally. Cut off the hard ends of the shimeji mushroom and separate. Peel and cut the carrots and daikon radish into 5mm thick rounds, using chrysanthemum shaped cutters, if you have them.

3. Put all ingredients and soup broth into an earthen pot and heat at medium, and add the daikon radishes and carrots when it starts to boil.

4. Add 1 when carrots and daikon radishes are heated through, along with the rest of the vegetables and shimeji. Start removing and eating the pieces as they become fully cooked.

POINTER!

火の通りにくい大根とにんじんをあらかじめしっかり煮ておく。

Thoroughly boil the daikon radishes and carrots beforehand.

水炊き
MIZUTAKI HOT POT

骨つきの肉を使って豪快に。
Use chicken with bones for a hearty meal.

322 kcal

1人分
One serving

材料 (4人分)

◎具
鶏骨つき肉 (ぶつ切り)··········800g
ねぎ·····························2本
わけぎ·························1束

◎だし
こぶ (10cm角)·················1枚
酒·················¼カップ (50ml)
水·····························適宜

◎つけだれ
ポン酢じょうゆ·················適宜

◎薬味
万能ねぎの小口切り、もみじおろし、
あらびき黒こしょう··········各適宜

作り方

1. 土なべにこぶと酒を入れて水を七
   分目まで注ぎ、20分ほどおく。

2. ねぎは斜め切りにし、わけぎは5～
   6cm長さに切る。

3. ①のなべを中火にかけ、煮立ったら
   鶏肉をそのまま入れ、アクをとりな
   がら20～30分煮る。鶏肉が煮え
   たら②を加える。煮えたものから、
   ポン酢じょうゆと好みの薬味で食べ
   る。

● つけだれで食べる 水炊き

　水炊きは湯やだしで仕立てるな
べ料理のことですが、ふつうは骨
つきの鶏ぶつ切り肉を使う鶏の水
炊きをさし、博多の名物料理とし
て知られています。だしやスープに
味をつけずにポン酢じょうゆなどの
つけだれで食べるのが特色です。
　骨つき肉からよい味のスープが
とれるので、最後に塩味にととのえ
て、しょうがやねぎなどの薬味を足
して味わうのも楽しみの一つです。

Ingredients (4 servings)

◎ Main ingredients
800g chicken with bone (cut into chunks)
2 naganegi onions
1 bunch wakegi green onions

◎ Soup stock
1 sheet kobu seaweed (10×10 cm)
¼ cup (50ml) sake
Water, as needed

◎ Dipping sauce
Ponzu, as needed

◎ Condiments
Chopped banno-negi onions, grated momiji daikon radish, crushed black pepper, as needed

Directions

1. Put the kobu and sake in an earthen pot, and fill up to 70% with water, then leave for about 20 minutes.

2. Cut the naganegi onions diagonally, and cut the wakegi green onions into 5 to 6cm lengths.

3. Heat 1 over medium. When it comes to a boil, add the chicken, remove the scum and simmer for 20 to 30 minutes. When the chicken is cooked, add 2. Eat with ponzu and condiments as the ingredients cook.

● Enjoy mizutaki hot pot with dipping sauce.

Mizutaki refers to cooking in hot water, which is usually a soup stock prepared with chunks of boned chicken.
　This dish is especially known as a specialty of the Hakata area. Instead of flavoring the soup stock or soup, the ingredients are flavored with a little dish of ponzu after they are removed from the pot.
　Because the boned meats release a nice flavor, finishing it with a salty taste and adding ginger, naganegi onions, and other condiments is another way to enjoy this meal.

POINTER!

鶏肉は骨つきのぶつ切りを使用する。骨からもだしが出るので、濃厚なスープになる。

Use chicken chunks with bones. The bones will add more broth to the soup and make it thick.

鶏肉から出るアクはこまめにすくいとる。

Carefully remove all the scum that comes out of the chicken.

たらちり

TARACHIRI COD HOT POT

淡白な白身魚をポン酢でさっぱりと味わう。
Enjoy the mild flavor of white fish with ponzu.

449 kcal

1人分
One serving

材料（4人分）

◎具
生たら・・・・・・・・・・・・・・・・・・・・・6切れ
白菜・・・・・・・・・・・・・・・・・・・・・・・・¼株
ねぎ・・・・・・・・・・・・・・・・・・・・・・・・・2本

◎だし
こぶ（10cm角）・・・・・・・・・・・・・・・ 1枚
酒・・・・・・・・・・・・・・・・ ¼カップ（50ml）
水・・・・・・・・・・・・・・・・・・・・・・・・・・適宜

◎つけだれ
ポン酢じょうゆ・・・・・・・・・・・・・・・・・適宜

◎薬味
万能ねぎの小口切り、もみじおろし
・・・・・・・・・・・・・・・・・・・・・・・・・・各適宜

作り方

1. 土なべにこぶと酒を入れて水を七分目まで注ぎ、20分ほどおく。

2. たらは大きめの一口大に切る。

3. 白菜は一口大に切る。ねぎは4〜5cm長さに切る。

4. ①を中火にかけ、煮立ったら②と③を入れ、煮えたものからポン酢じょうゆと好みの薬味で食べる。

🔍 水煮してたれで 食べるのがちりなべ

　ちりなべとは、魚貝類、主に白身魚を豆腐や野菜といっしょに煮て、ポン酢じょうゆなどのつけだれと薬味で食べる料理のこと。つまり本来は海鮮なべだったようです。

　しかし近年では材料にこだわらず、しょうゆやみそなどの調味料で味をつけずに水やだしだけで煮るなべをちりなべと総称するようになりました。

Ingredients (4 servings)

◎ Main ingredients
6 fresh cod pieces
¼ Napa Chinese cabbage
2 naganegi onions

◎ Soup stock
1 piece kobu seaweed (10×10cm)
¼ cup (50ml) sake
Water, as needed

◎ Dipping sauce
Ponzu, as needed

◎ Condiments
Chopped banno-negi onions, grated momiji daikon radish, as needed

Directions

1. Put the kobu seaweed and sake in an earthen pot, and fill to 70% with water, then let sit for about 20 minutes.

2. Cut the cod into large bite-size pieces.

3. Cut the Napa Chinese cabbage into bite-size pieces. Cut the onions into 4 or 5cm lengths.

4. Place 1 over medium heat. When it starts to boil, add 2 and 3. When cooked, eat with ponzu and your choice of condiments.

🔍 For chiri-nabe, simply boil ingredients in water and prepare a dipping sauce

Chiri-nabe refers to a dish made by boiling seafood, mostly white fish, with tofu and vegetables. The boiled food is then eaten by dipping bite-size portions in a sauce made of ponzu mixed with condiments. It was originally a seafood hot pot.

　These days, chiri-nabe is the collective term for all hot pots, regardless of the ingredients used. This includes hot pots garnished with soy sauce, miso and other condiments, as well as those made with only water or soup stock.

ほうれんそうと油揚げのみそ汁

DEEP-FRIED TOFU AND SPINACH MISO SOUP

みそを加えたら煮立たせないのが風味よく仕上げるコツ。
The key is not to let it boil after you add the miso in order to round out the flavors.

61 kcal
1人分
One serving

Ingredients (2 servings)

100g spinach
½ slice abura-age (deep-fried tofu)
1 ¾ cups (350ml) soup stock
1.5 tbsp (22.5ml) miso

Directions

1. Blanch the spinach in boiling water and squeeze out the excess water. Cut into 3cm lengths.

2. Pour boiling water onto the deep-fried tofu to remove some of the oil. Cut in half, then cut into 7 to 8mm widths.

3. Pour the soup stock in a pot and heat, then add the deep-fried tofu. When it starts to boil, add the spinach and cook.

4. Mix in the miso with the soup stock. Just before it boils, turn the heat off.

材料（2人分）

ほうれんそう ……………… 100g
油揚げ ………………………… ½枚
だし ………… 1 ¾ カップ (350ml)
みそ ………… 大さじ1.5 (22.5ml)

作り方

1. ほうれんそうは熱湯でさっとゆでて水けをしぼり、3cm長さに切る。

2. 油揚げは熱湯をかけて油抜きする。縦半分にし、7〜8mm幅に切る。

3. なべにだしを入れて火にかけ、油揚げを入れる。煮立ったらほうれんそうを加え、一煮する。

4. みそをだしでときのばして加え、沸騰前に火を止める。

POINTER!

みそを入れてグラグラ煮立てたり、煮すぎると風味がとんで塩辛さだけが口に残るので、みそは最後にとき入れて沸騰直前に火を止めます。

If you put in the miso and boil or overcook it, the flavor will disappear and it will leave a salty taste in your mouth. So, be sure to turn off the heat after adding the miso just before it boils.

玉ねぎとじゃがいものみそ汁
ONION AND POTATO MISO SOUP

だしでじゃがいもがやわらくなるまで煮てから、玉ねぎを加えます。
Cook the potato in the soup stock until it gets soft, then add the onions.

82 kcal
1人分
One serving

Ingredients (2 servings)

½ onion
1 potato
1 ¾ cups (350ml) soup stock
1.5 tbsp (22.5ml) miso

Directions

1. Cut the potato into 7-8mm thick quarters, rinse with water and drain. Cut the onion into wedges.

2. Pour the soup stock into a pot, and cook the potatoes. When tender, add the onions and heat through.

3. Add the miso and mix in the soup stock, and turn the heat off just before boiling.

🔍 クッキングメモ / COOKING MEMO

こんな組み合わせも美味
みそ汁は実の組み合わせがマンネリにならないように変化をつけて。キャベツ+絹さや、豚肉+にら、じゃがいも+わかめ、ピーマン+かぼちゃ、かぼちゃ+みょうが、オクラ+玉ねぎ、なす+さやいんげん、セロリ+トマト、かぶ+鶏ささ身、さつまいも+しめじ、まいたけ+れんこん、なめこ+豆腐、大根+油揚げ。

These ingredients also go well with each other for delicious variations.
So that you don't get tired of having the same ingredients in your miso soup, try different combinations. Examples are cabbage with snow peas, pork with garlic chives, potato with wakame seaweed, green pepper with pumpkin, pumpkin with myoga, okra with onion, eggplant with green beans, celery with tomato, turnip with chicken fillet, sweet potato with shimeji mushrooms, maitake mushrooms with lotus root, nameko mushrooms with tofu, daikon radish with abura-age (deep-fried tofu) and so on.

材料（2人分）

玉ねぎ ………………………… ½個
じゃがいも ……………………… 1個
だし ………… 1 ¾ カップ（350ml）
みそ ………… 大さじ1.5（22.5ml）

作り方

1. じゃがいもは7～8mm厚さのいちょう切りにし、水にさらして水けをきる。玉ねぎはくし形切りにする。

2. なべにだしを入れて火にかけ、じゃがいもを入れて煮る。やわらかくなったら玉ねぎを加えて火を通す。

3. みそをだしでときのばして加え、沸騰直前に火を止める。

豚汁

TON-JIRU (PORK AND VEGETABLE SOUP)

ボリュームも栄養も満点のおかずになる汁物。
A perfect side dish soup full of nutrition and filling.

221 kcal

1人分
One serving

Ingredients (2 servings)

100g thinly sliced pork meat
100g daikon radish
½ carrot
½ block konnyaku
½ tbsp (7.5ml) salad oil
2 tbsp (30ml) miso
½ naganegi onion

Directions

1. Cut the daikon radish and carrot into 3 to 4mm thick quarters. Tear the konnyaku into small pieces with a spoon and boil.

2. Heat the salad oil and cook the pork meat. When the meat turns color, add 1 and stir-fry.

3. When the oil has been absorbed, add 2 cups (400ml) of water. When it comes to a boil, turn to low heat and simmer till tender while removing the scum.

4. Mix in and add the miso with a small amount of cooking soup, then sprinkle the sliced naganegi onions.

POINTER!

水分が多くて味のしみにくいこんにゃくですが、スプーンなどで一口大にちぎると、煮汁にふれる面積が多くなるので、味がしみやすくなります。

Konnyaku has a lot of moisture and doesn't easily absorb flavors. Tear it into bite-size pieces with a spoon to create more surface area for the flavor to soak into.

材料 (2人分)

豚こまぎれ肉‥‥‥‥‥‥‥100g
大根‥‥‥‥‥‥‥‥‥‥‥‥100g
にんじん‥‥‥‥‥‥‥‥‥‥½本
こんにゃく‥‥‥‥‥‥‥‥‥½枚
サラダ油‥‥‥‥大さじ½ (7.5ml)
みそ‥‥‥‥‥‥大さじ2 (30ml)
ねぎ‥‥‥‥‥‥‥‥‥‥‥‥½本

作り方

1. 大根、にんじんは3〜4mm厚さのいちょう切りにする。こんにゃくはスプーンでちぎって下ゆでする。

2. サラダ油を熱して豚肉を炒め、肉の色が変わったら①を加えて炒める。

3. 全体に油がなじんだら、水2カップ (400ml)を加える。煮立ったら弱火にしてアクをとり、やわらかくなるまで煮る。

4. みそを煮汁少々でときのばして加え、ねぎの小口切りを散らす。

ぶりのかす汁
LEES AND YELLOWTAIL SOUP

ぶりと酒かすのうまみとコクで、体のしんからあたたまる実だくさんの汁物。

Enjoy this soup full of ingredients and the rich flavor of yellowtail and sake lees that will warm you to the core.

371 kcal
1人分
One serving

Ingredients (2 servings)

2 yellowtail fish
100g daikon radish
½ carrot

A | 100g ita sake lees
  | ½ cup (100ml) soup stock
  | 2 tbsp (30ml) miso

1 ¼ cups (250ml) soup stock
Mitsuba trefoil, to your taste

Directions

1. Tear the sake lees into small pieces and soak in the soup stock, then mix in the miso.
2. Cut the yellowtail in half.
3. Cut the daikon radish and carrot into rectangles.
4. Put the soup stock over high and when it starts to boil, add in the yellowtail. When it starts to boil again, turn the heat to medium and remove the scum, add 3 and cook for 7 to 8 minutes.
5. Add 1 and mix in, and then sprinkle on the mitsuba trefoil (cut in 3cm lengths).

なべ・汁もの
Hot Soup

材料（2人分）

ぶりの切り身……………2切れ
大根………………………100g
にんじん………………… ½本

A | 酒かす(板かす)………100g
  | だし……… ½カップ(100ml)
  | みそ……… 大さじ2 (30ml)

だし………1 ¼カップ(250ml)
三つ葉……………………少々

作り方

1. Aの酒かすは小さくちぎってだしにひたし、みそを合わせてとく。
2. ぶりは半分に切る。
3. 大根、にんじんは短冊切りにする。
4. だしを強火にかけ、煮立ったらぶりを入れる。再び煮立ったら中火にしてアクをとり、③を加えて7～8分煮る。
5. ①を加えて煮とかし、3cm長さに切った三つ葉を散らす。

POINTER!

酒かす（板かす）は、平らな形をしているので、最初に小さくちぎってだしにひたしておくと、やわらかくなってみそと合わせやすくなります。

Because the ita sake lees is flat shaped, first tear into small pieces. Letting them soak until soft will make it easier to mix them into the miso.

けんちん汁

KENCHIN-JIRU SOUP
(TOFU WITH BURDOCK AND SESAME OIL)

豆腐の水けがとぶまで炒めるのがコツ。
The key is to cook the tofu until all the moisture is cooked out of it.

104 kcal
1人分
One serving

Ingredients (2 servings)

½ pack firm tofu
¼ burdock
½ tbsp (7.5ml) sesame oil
2 cups (400ml) soup stock
Salt, to your taste
Soy sauce, to your taste

Directions

1. Break up the tofu by hand and place on a strainer. Let it drain for 10 minutes.

2. Scrape the skin of the burdock and cut into long thin shavings, then rinse in water for 10 minutes. Drain the water.

3. Heat the sesame oil in a pot, then cook the tofu. When all the water is cooked out, add the burdock and cook until tender.

4. Add the soup stock and cook for 5 or 6 minutes. When the burdock is tender, add salt and soy sauce to taste.

POINTER!

豆腐はごま油でよく炒めます。こうすることで豆腐の余分な水分がとんで、ごぼうのうまみも吸収しやすく、コクのある仕上がりになります。

Cook the tofu well in sesame oil. That way the excess water from the tofu is cooked out, and it can better absorb the umami flavor of the burdock, giving it a rich taste.

材料 (2人分)

木綿豆腐 ………………… ½丁
ごぼう ………………… ¼本
ごま油 ……… 大さじ½ (7.5ml)
だし ………… 2 カップ (400ml)
塩 …………………… 少々
しょうゆ ………………… 少々

作り方

1. 豆腐は手でくずしてざるに入れ、10分おいて水けをきる。

2. ごぼうは皮をこそげてささがきにし、水に10分さらして水けをきる。

3. なべにごま油を熱して豆腐を炒める。水分がとんだら、ごぼうを加えてしんなりするまでさらに炒める。

4. だしを加えて5〜6分煮る。ごぼうがやわらかくなったら、塩、しょうゆで味をととのえる。

いわしのつみれ汁

SARDINE TSUMIRE-JIRU (MINCED SARDINE SOUP)

アクをていねいにすくいとることで、汁を濁らせずすっきりとした仕上がりに。
Carefully remove scum to make a nice, clear soup.

184 kcal
1人分
One serving

Ingredients (2 servings)

2 sardines

A | 8cm naganegi onion
 | 1 ginger piece
 | 1 tbsp (15ml) sake
 | Salt, to your taste

B | 1 ¾ cups (350ml) water
 | ¼ cup (50ml) sake

Salt, to your taste
1 naganegi onion stalk

Directions

1. Finely chop the naganegi onion and ginger from A. Cut the leftover naganegi onion into thin diagonal slices.

2. Tebiraki (split open with your hands) the sardines, remove the spine and small bones, and chop finely. Add the naganegi onions, ginger, sake, and salt from A, then chop with a knife until it's minced.

3. Put B into a pot and turn the heat to high. When it starts to boil, scoop 2 with a spoon, shape, and then drop it in.

4. When it starts to boil again, turn down the heat and remove the scum, and cook until the tsumire (minced fish) starts to float. When cooked through, add salt to taste and sprinkle on the naganegi onions.

なべ・汁もの
Hot Soup

材料（2人分）

いわし ……………………… 2尾

A | ねぎ ……………………… 8cm
 | しょうが ………………… 1かけ
 | 酒 ………………… 大さじ1 (15ml)
 | 塩 ………………………… 少々

B | 水 ………… 1¾カップ (350ml)
 | 酒 …………… ¼カップ (50ml)

塩 ………………………… 少々
ねぎ ……………………… 1本

作り方

1. Aのねぎ、しょうがはみじん切りにする。残りのねぎは斜め薄切りにしておく。

2. いわしは手開きにし、中骨と腹骨をとってこまかく刻む。Aのねぎ、しょうが、酒、塩を加えてまぜ、包丁でたたいてすり身状にする。

3. なべにBを入れて強火にかける。煮立ったら、②をスプーンですくって形をととのえ、落とし入れる。

4. 再び煮立ったら火を弱めてアクをとり、つみれが浮いてくるまで煮る。火が通ったら塩で味をととのえて、ねぎを散らす。

POINTER!

薬味野菜をたっぷり加えてたたきます。つみれはスプーン2本を使うと形をととのえやすく、手も汚れません。

Add a lot of spicy vegetables and chop. Use two spoons to scoop and to form the tsumire (minced fish), and your hands won't get messy.

焼き鶏
YAKITORI (CHICKEN SKEWER)

香ばしい香りと甘辛しょうゆ味でうまさ倍増。
Savory aroma enhanced by the salty-sweet soy sauce flavor.

304 kcal
1人分
One serving

材料（2〜3人分）

鶏もも肉··················1枚（200g）

◎たれ

しょうゆ ·············½カップ（100ml）

みりん ·············½カップ（100ml）

砂糖 ·················大さじ½（7.5ml）

ねぎ（青い部分）················10cm

しょうがの薄切り··················2枚

※竹ぐし（12cm 長さぐらい）はあらかじめ
水に浸して湿らせておく。

作り方

1. たれの材料をなべに入れ、弱火で
30分煮詰める。

2. 鶏肉は皮を上にし、もものつけ根の
方から皮をひっぱりながら、皮のくっ
ついているところに包丁を入れては
がす。脂肪があればとり除き、2〜
3cm角に切り揃える。

3. まな板の手前端に鶏肉を置き、上面
をしっかり押さえて、まな板と並行に
くしを刺す。1本に4切れずつ刺し、
竹ぐしの先端は出しておく。竹ぐしを
刺すときは力を込めるので、手を刺
さないように注意すること。

4. コンロに焼き網をのせ、「遠火の強
火」ができるように焼き台を工夫し
（写真は、大型のアルミ製のパウン
ド型の底を切りとって焼き網にセッ
ト）、③を並べる。

5. 遠火の強火で焼く。焼き台の端の
方は炎が届きにくいので、くしの場
所を入れ替えながら焼くとよい。

6. 下側の肉の色が変わってきたら裏
返し、肉全体の色が変わったら火
からはずし、①のたれを全体に塗る。

7. ⑥を焼き台に戻し、乾いたらたれを
塗る、を繰り返してこんがりと焼き
上げる。

Ingredients (2-3 servings)

1 (200g) chicken thigh

◎ sauce

½ cup (100ml) soy sauce

½ cup (100ml) mirin (sweet sake)

½ tbsp (7.5ml) sugar

10cm naganegi onion (green end)

2 thin ginger slices

※ Bamboo skewers (about 12cm long)
pre-soaked in water

Directions

1. Put all the sauce ingredients in a pot. Heat
on low and boil down for 30 minutes.

2. Place the chicken skin side up onto a cutting board. Then grab the skin from the
end of the thigh and by using a knife to
cut, pull and remove. Remove excess fat
and dice the chicken into 2-3cm uniform
cubes.

3. Place the chicken at the front edge of the
cutting board, hold firm and skewer the
chicken. Skewer 4 pieces on one skewer
and leave the end of the bamboo showing.
You will use a lot of force when skewering,
so be careful not to poke yourself.

4. Place the grill on the burner and adjust it
so you can roast the chicken at a high temperature, but a good distance from the
flame. (In the picture, a cooking grate has
been placed on a large aluminum baking
pan whose bottom has been cut out.)
Place on 3.

5. Roast on high heat, but far enough away
from the fire. Since it is hard to get the
ends and sides of the roasting rack properly heated, it is better to alternate the
placement of all the skewers when roasting.

6. When the bottom of the chicken starts to
turn color, turn over, and when all the sides
have turned color, remove from the heat
and baste the sauce from 1 all around.

7. Place 6 back onto the roasting rack. Baste
when the sauce dries and repeat until it is
nicely roasted.

鶏肉の照り焼き

CHICKEN TERIYAKI SLATHERED WITH TARE SAUCE

おいしさのコツは、鶏肉の両面をフォークでつついて穴をあけ、火の通りや味のしみ込みをよくします。

The key to a good chicken teriyaki is to use a fork to poke the chicken on both sides so that it cooks better and absorbs more flavor.

265 kcal
1人分
One serving

78

材料（2人分）

鶏もも肉（または胸肉）…1枚（200g）

A | しょうゆ………… 大さじ1（15ml）
　 | みりん…………… 大さじ1（15ml）

サラダ油…………… 大さじ½（7.5ml）
ししとうがらし ………………… 10本

> 皮は力を入れてブスリ、ブスリ！
> Put some muscle into it and stab the skin!

作り方

1. 鶏肉は両面をフォークで刺して穴を
   あける。こうしておけば焼き縮みも
   少なく、味のしみ込みもよくなる。

2. Aを合わせて鶏肉をつけ、もみ込む
   ようにして味をなじませる。このまま
   10分おき、ときどき上下を返す。

3. ししとうは炒めたとき破裂しないよう
   に、竹ぐしを刺して穴をあけ、サラ
   ダ油でさっと炒めてとり出す。

4. 鶏肉の汁けをきり、皮目を下にして
   同じフライパンに入れ、強火でこん
   がりと焼きつけて裏返す。

5. 鶏肉の両面にこんがりと焼き色がつ
   いたら中火にし、ふたをして4〜5
   分蒸し焼きにする。

6. 強火に戻して残ったつけ汁を加え、
   照りよくからめて焼く。食べやすく切
   って器に盛り、ししとうを添える。

Ingredients (2 servings)

1 (200g) chicken thigh (or breast)

A | 1 tbsp (15ml) soy sauce
　 | 1 tbsp (15ml) mirin (sweet sake)

½ tbsp (7.5ml) salad oil
10 whole shishito peppers

Directions

1. Poke holes into the surface of the chicken with a fork. That way, it won't shrink and will absorb more flavor when cooked.

2. Mix the ingredients in A and marinate the chicken. Blend the flavors into the chicken by rubbing. Leave for 10 minutes and turn over from time to time.

3. To prevent the shishito peppers from splitting, poke a hole in them with a skewer and lightly pan fry with salad oil, then take out.

4. Remove the excess moisture from the chicken. Use the same frying pan and place the skin side down. Heat over high heat till golden brown and turn over.

5. When both sides of the chicken turn golden brown, turn the heat down to medium and cover. Steam cook for 4 to 5 minutes.

6. Turn the heat back to high and add the leftover marinade and sauce it well onto the chicken. Cut into bite-size pieces and place on a serving dish, then add the shishito peppers.

> ここでしっかり中まで火を通す
> Make sure to heat all the way through.

いり鶏

CHICKEN BOILED WITH VEGETABLES

炒めた鶏肉から出たコクと、れんこんのシャキシャキッとした歯ざわりが絶妙。
The flavor of the cooked chicken and the texture of the lotus root are a perfect match.

390 kcal
1人分
One serving

材料（2人分）

鶏もも肉	‥‥‥‥‥‥‥	1枚（200g）
にんじん	‥‥‥‥‥‥‥	大1本
れんこん	‥‥‥‥‥‥	200g
ごま油	‥‥‥‥‥	大さじ½（7.5ml）

A	酒	‥‥‥‥‥	大さじ2（30ml）
	水	‥‥‥‥‥	1カップ（200ml）
	砂糖	‥‥‥‥	大さじ½（7.5ml）
	塩	‥‥‥‥	小さじ¼（1.25ml）
	しょうゆ	‥‥‥	大さじ1（15ml）
	みりん	‥‥‥‥	大さじ1（15ml）

作り方

1. 鶏肉は一口大に切る。にんじんは乱切りにし、れんこんは乱切りにして水に7〜8分さらして水けをきる。

2. フライパンにごま油を熱して、強火で鶏肉を焼きつけるように炒める。

3. 鶏肉の表面にこんがりと焼き色がついたら、にんじん、れんこんを加えて炒め合わせる。

4. 全体に油がなじんだらAの酒、水、砂糖、塩、しょうゆ、みりんの順に加える。

5. 煮立ったら中火にし、ときどき上下を入れかえるようにまぜ、ほとんど汁けがなくなるまで12〜13分煮る。

Ingredients (2 servings)

1 (200g) chicken thigh
1 large carrot
200g lotus root
½ tbsp (7.5ml) sesame oil

A | 2 tbsp (30ml) sake
1 cup (200ml) water
½ tbsp (7.5ml) sugar
¼ tsp (1.25ml) salt
1 tbsp (15ml) soy sauce
1 tbsp (15ml) mirin (sweet sake)

Directions

1. Cut the chicken into bite-size pieces. Cut the carrot and lotus root into chunks and soak in water for 7 to 8 minutes, then drain.

2. Heat sesame oil on a frying pan over high heat and fry the chicken.

3. When the chicken turns golden brown, add the carrots and lotus roots and stir fry.

4. When the oil has been absorbed, add A in this order: sake, water, sugar, salt, soy sauce, and mirin.

5. When it starts to boil, turn the heat down to medium, mixing occasionally to bring the bottom ingredients to the top, and simmer for 12 to 13 minutes till the moisture is almost gone.

アレンジ | Variations こんにゃくを加えて

材料（2人分）

鶏もも肉1枚（200g）、にんじん1本、れんこん150g、こんにゃく1本、ごま油大さじ½（7.5ml）、酒大さじ2（30ml）、だし⅓カップ（約67ml）、砂糖・しょうゆ・みりん各大さじ1（15ml）、塩小さじ½（2.5ml）、木の芽少々

作り方

こんにゃくは大きめの一口大に切って水から下ゆでする。れんこんとにんじんを炒めるときにこんにゃくもいっしょに入れ、あとは調味して煮る。仕上げに木の芽をのせる。

ADD THE KONNYAKU

Ingredients (2 servings)

1 (200g) chicken thigh
1 large carrot
150g lotus root
1 block konnyaku
½ tbsp (7.5ml) sesami oil
2 tbsp (30ml) sake
⅓ cup (about 67ml) soup stock
1 tbsp (15ml) each sugar, soy sauce, mirin (sweet sake)
½ tsp (2.5ml) salt
Leaf buds, as needed

Directions

Cut the konnyaku into large bite-size pieces and boil in water. Stir-fry the lotus root and carrot, and add the konnyaku. Season and simmer. Serve garnished with leaf buds.

鶏肉の蒸し焼き・薬味だれ
STEAMED CHICKEN WITH SPICY SAUCE

ふっくら蒸し焼きにした鶏肉に、ごま、酢を加えた薬味だれをたっぷりかけたメニューです。
A hearty dish with steamed chicken and a slather of sesame and vinegar spice sauce added.

305 kcal
1人分
One serving

材料 (2人分)

鶏もも肉 (または胸肉) …1枚 (200g)

A | 塩 …………………………… 少々
　 | 酒 ……………… 大さじ1 (15ml)

サラダ油 ………… 大さじ½ (7.5ml)
酒 ………………………大さじ1 (15ml)

B | ねぎ ……………………………5cm
　 | しょうが ………………… 1かけ
　 | しょうゆ ………… 大さじ1 (15ml)
　 | 切り白ごま………大さじ1 (15ml)
　 | 砂糖 ………… 小さじ1.5 (7.5ml)
　 | 酢 ……………… 大さじ1 (15ml)
　 | ごま油 ………… 小さじ½ (2.5ml)

作り方

1. 鶏肉は両面をフォークで刺して穴を
   あけ、Aを加えてもみ込むようにし
   て下味をつける。

2. フライパンにサラダ油を熱して鶏肉
   を皮目を下にして入れ、強火で焼き
   つける。

3. こんがりとしたら、酒を振り入れてふ
   たをし、中火で7〜8分蒸し焼きに
   して火を通す。

4. Bのねぎ、しょうがはみじん切りにし、
   ほかのBを加えてまぜる。

5. 鶏肉のあら熱がとれたら、一口大に
   切って器に盛り、④の薬味だれをか
   ける。

🔍 クッキングメモ

**「酒」は素材をおいしくしてくれる
優秀な調味料**

酒は肉や魚のくさみを消すだけでなく、
素材をやわらかくしたり、うまみをしみ
込ませたり、仕上げに加えるとまろや
かにと、用途に応じて幅広い働きをし
てくれるので和食には欠かせない調味
料の一つです。料理酒には調味料が
入っているのでできれば「清酒」を。

Ingredients (2 servings)

1 (200g) chicken thigh (or breast)

A | Salt, to your taste
　 | 1 tbsp (15ml) sake

½ tbsp (7.5ml) salad oil
1 tbsp (15ml) sake

B | 5cm naganegi onion
　 | 1 piece ginger
　 | 1 tbsp (15ml) soy sauce
　 | 1 tbsp (15ml) chopped white sesame
　 | 1.5 tsp (7.5ml) sugar
　 | 1 tbsp (15ml) vinegar
　 | ½ tsp (2.5ml) sesame oil

Directions

1. Poke the surface of the chicken on both
   sides with a fork, add the ingredients in A
   and marinate by rubbing it in.

2. Heat the salad oil on a frying pan over
   high and cook skin-side down.

3. When it turns golden brown, add the sake,
   cover, and steam cook over medium heat
   for 7 to 8 minutes to cook through.

4. Finely chop the naganegi onion and ginger
   in B, add the rest of the ingredients in B
   and mix.

5. After letting the chicken sit for a while, cut
   into bite-size pieces and serve with 4.

🔍 COOKING MEMO

**Sake is a great ingredient for enhan-
cing the flavor of other ingredients**

Sake not only removes the bad smell of
meat and fish, but it also makes them tender and infuses umami flavor when added
to finish. Depending on its use, sake plays
a big role and is one of the most important
ingredients in Japanese cooking. There are
flavoring agents in cooking sake, so try to
use refined sake.

鶏肉の立田揚げ

TATSUTA FRIED CHICKEN

揚げ物もフライパンを使えば、少ない油でしかも簡単に揚げられます。
You can easily fry foods using a frying pan with a small amount of oil.

428 kcal
1人分
One serving

材料（2人分）

鶏もも肉 …………… 大1枚 (250g)

A｜しょうゆ ………… 大さじ1 (15ml)
　｜酒 ……………… 大さじ½ (7.5ml)
　｜みりん ………… 大さじ½ (7.5ml)

かたくり粉 ………………………… 適宜
揚げ油 …………………………… 適宜
すだち …………………………… 適宜

作り方

1. 鶏肉は余分な皮と脂肪を少しそぎとる。両面をフォークで刺して穴をあけ、大きめの一口大に切る。

2. Aを合わせて鶏肉をつけ、もみ込むようにして味をなじませる。このまま15分おき、ときどき上下を返す。

3. 鶏肉をペーパータオルではさんで、汁けをよくふきとる。

4. 揚げる直前に、鶏肉にかたくり粉をまんべんなくまぶして、余分な粉をはたき落とす。

5. 揚げ油を170～180度に熱して鶏肉を入れ、途中で返してこんがりと色よく揚げ、中まで火を通す。

6. ペーパータオルを敷いて⑤の立田揚げをのせ、油をよくきる。器に盛って半分に切ったすだちを添える。

🔍 クッキングメモ

お弁当のおかずにも最適

カラッと香ばしく揚がった「鶏肉の立田揚げ」は、ごはんのおかずや酒の肴にもおすすめです。中までしっかり味がついていて、冷めてもおいしいので、多めに作って次の日のお弁当にどうぞ。

Ingredients (2 servings)

1 large piece (250g) chicken thigh

A｜1 tbsp (15ml) soy sauce
　｜½ tbsp (7.5ml) sake
　｜½ tbsp (7.5ml) mirin (sweet sake)

Potato starch, as needed
Frying oil, as needed
Sudachi citrus, as needed

> このひと手間でカラッと揚がる
> This will make the chicken crispy.

Directions

1. Remove a bit of the excess fat and skin from the chicken. Poke holes on both sides with a fork and cut into large bite-size pieces.

2. Mix the ingredients in A and pour it on the chicken. Rub it in to marinate. Leave for 15 minutes and occasionally turn over.

3. Wrap the chicken with paper towels and damp dry.

4. Just before frying, coat the chicken with potato starch and dust off the excess powder.

5. Heat the frying oil to between 170 and 180 degrees, then put the chicken pieces in, turn them over, cook through, and fry till golden brown.

6. Place the 5 (tatsuta fried chicken) on paper towels to soak the excess oil. Serve garnished with a sudachi citrus cut in half.

🔍 COOKING MEMO

A perfect side dish for an obento lunch

The crispy tatsuta fried chicken is a perfect accompaniment for rice or sake. Because it is well marinated and tastes good even when cold, you can make extras and use the leftovers for the following day's obento lunch.

肉のおかず
Meat Dishes

鶏ささ身の治部煮

JIBU-NI BOILED CHICKEN FILLET

鶏ささ身はそば粉をつけながら煮立った煮汁に入れると、つるんとしたなめらかな口当たりに。
If you apply buckwheat flour to the chicken fillets while cooking them in the boiling soup broth,
the texture of the chicken will become smooth and nice.

209 kcal
1人分
One serving

材料（2人分）

鶏ささ身（筋なし）………4本（200g）
にんじん……………………… 小½本
絹さや ……………………………50g
そば粉……大さじ2～3（30～45ml）
しょうゆ……………… 小さじ1（5ml）

A｜だし ………… 1.5 カップ（300ml）
　｜酒………………… 大さじ2（30ml）
　｜みりん………… 大さじ1（15ml）
　｜砂糖…………… 小さじ1（5ml）
　｜塩 ……………… 小さじ½（2.5ml）
　｜しょうゆ……… 大さじ½（7.5ml）

ねりわさび…………………… 少々

全体に下味をさっとからめる →
Marinate thoroughly

作り方

1. にんじんは3cm長さ、1cm幅の短冊切りにする。絹さやは筋をとる。

2. ささ身は一口大のそぎ切りにし、しょうゆを振り入れて下味をつける。

3. Aを合わせて火にかけ、にんじんを入れる。煮立ったら、ささ身にそば粉をはたきつけながら加える。

4. 5～6分煮て火が通ったら、絹さやを加えて一煮する。器に汁ごと盛り、わさびをのせる。

🔍 クッキングメモ

「治部煮」とは

治部煮は、加賀の代表的な料理で、かもを使うのが有名です。昔金沢城が完成したとき祝いの宴に出されたのが始まりと伝えられています。ほかに「じぶじぶと煮る」からなど由来はさまざまですが、ここでは鶏ささ身を使って手軽に。下味をつけたささ身にそば粉（なければ小麦粉）をはたきつけながら煮汁に落とし入れます。あとは「じぶじぶと煮る」だけでしっかり味がからみます。

Ingredients (2 servings)

4 chicken fillets, without sinew (200g)
½ small carrot
50g snow peas
2 to 3 tbsp (30-45ml) buckwheat flour
1 tsp (5ml) soy sauce

A｜1.5 cups (300ml) soup stock
　｜2 tbsp (30ml) sake
　｜1 tbsp (15ml) mirin (sweet sake)
　｜1 tsp (5ml) sugar
　｜½ tsp (2.5ml) salt
　｜½ tbsp (7.5ml) soy sauce

Wasabi paste, to your taste

Directions

1. Slice the carrot into rectangles (1 x 3cm). String the snow peas.

2. Cut the fillets into bite-size diagonal pieces and marinate in soy sauce.

3. Mix the ingredients in A and heat. Put the carrots in. When it starts to boil, dust on the buckwheat flour.

4. Cook for 5 to 6 minutes and when everything is heated through, add the snow peas and boil. Serve in a dish with the soup and add wasabi on top.

🔍 COOKING MEMO

What is a jibu-ni?

Jibu-ni is a staple of the Kaga area, where duck is often used. It is said to have been served for the first time at a feast celebrating the completion of the Kanazawa Castle in ancient days. Another possible origin of the name may be the boiling sound. The recipe here calls for chicken fillets. Dust buckwheat flour (or wheat flour) into the broth. After that, simply leave it to simmer as the flavors are absorbed.

鶏手羽先とごぼうの煮物

CHICKEN WINGS AND BURDOCK BOILED DISHES

手羽先は煮る前に表面をこんがりと焼きつけるのが、おいしさのポイント。
The key is to fry to golden brown before simmering.

257 kcal
1人分
One serving

材料 (2人分)

鶏手羽先 ……………………… 6本
ごぼう ……………………… 1本
ごま油 ………… 大さじ½ (7.5ml)

A | 酒 ……………… 大さじ3 (45ml)
　 | 湯 ……………… 2カップ (400ml)
　 | みりん ………… 大さじ1 (15ml)
　 | しょうゆ ……… 大さじ2 (30ml)

作り方

1. ごぼうは皮をこそげて4cm長さに切り、さらに縦半分にする。水にさらして10分おき、水けをよくきる。

2. 手羽先は裏側の骨に沿って切り込みを入れる。こうしておけば火の通りもよく、味がしみ込みやすい。

3. フライパンにごま油を熱して手羽先を焼きつける。こんがりと焼き色がついたらごぼうを加えて炒める。

4. 油がなじんだらAの酒を振り入れ、湯、みりん、しょうゆの順に加えて調味する。

5. 煮立ったら弱火にしてアクをていねいにとり、落としぶたをして煮る。

6. ときどき上下を入れかえるようにまぜ、ほとんど汁けがなくなるまで25〜30分煮る。

> 煮汁が回るように落としぶたを
> A drop lid helps to make sure ingredients have an even flavor.

Ingredients (2 servings)

6 chicken wings
1 burdock
½ tbsp (7.5ml) sesame oil

A | 3 tbsp (45ml) sake
　 | 2 cups (400ml) hot water
　 | 1 tbsp (15ml) mirin (sweet sake)
　 | 2 tbsp (30ml) soy sauce

> 包丁の先で裏側にだけ入れる
> Only make incisions on the back using the point of the knife.

Directions

1. Scrape the skin of the burdock and cut into 4cm lengths, then cut in half lengthwise. Soak in water and leave for 10 minutes. Drain well.

2. Make small incisions along the bones on the other side of the chicken wings. That way, it will cook better and absorb more flavor.

3. Heat sesame oil in a frying pan, then pan sear the chicken wings. When they turn golden brown, add the burdock and cook.

4. When the oil has been absorbed, pour the sake from A, then add the hot water, mirin, and soy sauce in that order to season.

5. When it starts to boil, turn the heat to low and carefully remove the scum, then place a drop lid and simmer.

6. Occasionally mix around, moving the ingredients at the bottom to the top, and simmer for 25 to 30 minutes until most of the liquid is cooked out.

肉のおかず
Meat Dishes

とんカツ
PORK CUTLET

ちょっとした下ごしらえのコツをマスターすれば、サクッとおいしく揚げられます。
Mastering a small step in the preparation stage will give you crispy and flavorful results!

508 kcal
1人分
One serving

材料 (2人分)

豚ロース肉 (とんかつ用) ………	2枚
塩 …………………………	少々
こしょう ………………………	少々
A ┌ 小麦粉 …………………	適宜
├ とき卵 …………………	適宜
└ パン粉 …………………	適宜
揚げ油 …………………………	適宜
とんかつソース ………………	適宜
キャベツ ………………………	適宜

作り方

1. キャベツはせん切りにし、冷水に7〜8分放してパリッとさせ、水けをきる。

2. 豚肉は筋切り (P.97) をする。全体を軽くたたいたあと、形を元に戻して塩、こしょうを振る。

3. パン粉に霧を吹いて生パン粉状にもどす。豚肉に小麦粉、とき卵、もどしたパン粉の順に衣をつける。

4. 揚げ油を170〜180度に熱して豚肉を入れる。途中で返してこんがりと色よく揚げ、中まで火を通す。

5. 油をよくきって食べやすく切る。器に盛ってキャベツを添え、好みでとんかつソースをかけて食べる。

🔎 クッキングメモ

**いつもの「とんカツ」を
ワンランクアップ！**

まず筋切りをして揚げたときに肉が縮むのを防ぎます。さらにやわらかくするために肉をたたいて伸ばし、手で形をととのえて元の大きさに戻します。パン粉は霧を吹いて生パン粉状にしてから使います。このちょっとしたコツを覚えておけば衣はサクッ、肉もやわらかい仕上がりに。

Ingredients (2 servings)

2 pieces pork loin meat (for cutlet)
Salt, to your taste
Pepper, to your taste

A | Flour, as needed
  | Beaten egg, as needed
  | Bread crumbs, as needed

Frying oil, as needed
Tonkatsu sauce, as needed
Cabbage, as needed

Directions

1. Finely slice the cabbage and immerse in ice water for 7 to 8 minutes to make it crispy fresh, and then drain.

2. Make incisions in the pork sinew (see page 97). After lightly pounding it, form it back into its original shape and season with salt and pepper.

3. Spray bread crumbs with water mist to turn them into raw bread crumbs. Coat the pork meat with flour, then the beaten egg, then the bread crumbs.

4. Heat the frying oil to between 170 and 180 degrees, then put the pork meat in. After it cooks for a while, turn it over and fry till golden brown, heating all the way through.

5. Let the oil drip off, then cut into bite-size pieces. Serve with finely sliced cabbage, and flavor with tonkatsu sauce.

🔎 COOKING MEMO

Make your tonkatsu a little special!

Make incisions in the meat, so that it doesn't shrink when you fry it. To make it more tender, pound out the meat and then form it back into its original shape. Use the bread crumbs after you spray them with mist water to turn them into raw bread-crumbs. Just remembering these pointers will make for a crispy batter and a tender meat finish.

豚つくねの焼き野菜添え

PORK TSUKUNE (KNEADED PORK) AND GRILLED VEGETABLES

つくねは七味をピリリときかせて塩味でさっぱりと。
Season tsukune with the spiciness of shichimi spice and refreshing saltiness.

207 kcal
1人分
One serving

材料（2人分）

豚ひき肉（赤身）················200g
グリーンアスパラガス···········4本
生しいたけ····················4個

A｜ねぎ·····················½本
　｜しょうが ················1かけ
　｜卵························1個
　｜塩··············小さじ¼（1.25ml）
　｜七味とうがらし·············少々

作り方

1. アスパラは根元のかたいところを2cmくらい切り落とす。しいたけは石づきを切りとる。

2. Aのねぎ、しょうがをみじん切りにし、ひき肉、ほかのAを合わせて粘りが出るまでよくまぜる。

3. 4等分にして、小判形に形をととのえる。

4. 焼き網を熱し、③のつくねを並べて焼く。こんがりと焼き色がついたら裏返して、中までしっかり火を通す。

5. アスパラ、しいたけを焼き網に並べて両面を焼く。食べやすく切って、つくねとともに盛り合わせる。

Ingredients (2 servings)

200g ground pork (lean)
4 stalks green asparagus
4 pieces raw shiitake mushroom

A｜½ naganegi onion
　｜1 piece ginger
　｜1 egg
　｜¼ tsp (1.25ml) salt
　｜Shichimi spice, to your taste

Directions

1. Cut off 2cm of the hard ends of the asparagus. Cut off the hard ends of the shiitake mushrooms.

2. Finely chop the naganegi onion and ginger from A, then combine the ground meat and the rest of the ingredients in A. Knead well until sticky.

3. Split into 4 equal parts, then form into oval shapes.

4. Heat the grill and cook the 3 (tsukune). When it starts to turn golden brown, turn it over and grill through.

5. Grill the asparagus and shiitake mushrooms on both sides on the grill. Cut into bite-size pieces and serve with tsukune.

豚肉のごましょうが焼き
GINGER SESAME PORK

強火で一気に焼いて肉汁を閉じ込め、仕上げにつけ汁をからめます。
Sear the meat quickly to lock in the flavors and finish by pouring on the sauce.

388 kcal
1人分
One serving

材料（2人分）

豚ロース肉（しょうが焼き用）…200g
しょうが……………………… 1かけ
切り白ごま………… 大さじ2（30ml）
A｜しょうゆ…… 大さじ1.5（22.5ml）
　｜酒 …………………大さじ1（15ml）
　｜みりん……………大さじ1（15ml）
サラダ油………… 大さじ½（7.5ml）
レタス……………………………… 適宜

作り方

1. Aのしょうゆ、酒、みりんを合わせてつけ汁を作る。ごまを入れ、しょうがをすりおろして加える。

2. 豚肉は筋切り（P.97）をして、つけ汁に広げて入れる。全体につけ汁をからめて10分ほどおく。

3. 豚肉に下味をつけている間に、レタスは一口大にちぎり、氷水に放してパリッとさせ、水けをよくきる。

4. サラダ油を熱し、豚肉の汁けを軽くきって1枚ずつ広げて入れ、強火でこんがりと焼きつけて裏返す。

5. 両面にこんがりと焼き色がついたら、残ったつけ汁を加えて全体にからめる。器に盛り、レタスを添える。

強火でうまみと肉汁を閉じ込める
Lock in the meat juices and umami by using high heat.

Ingredients (2 servings)

200g pork loin (cut for ginger pork)
1 piece ginger
2 tbsp (30ml) chopped white sesame

A | 1.5 tbsp (22.5ml) soy sauce
  | 1 tbsp (15ml) sake
  | 1 tbsp (15ml) mirin (sweet sake)

½ tbsp (7.5ml) salad oil
Lettuce, as needed.

Directions

1. Mix the ingredients in A to make the sauce. Put the sesame in and add the grated ginger.

2. Make incisions into the pork (see page 97), then place inside the sauce to marinate. Leave to marinate for 10 minutes after fully covering in the sauce.

3. While you are marinating the pork, cut the lettuce into bite-size pieces and let it sit in ice water to crisp it up, then drain well.

4. Heat the salad oil. Let the marinade drip off a bit, spread each piece one by one. Then place the meat on a pan over high. Cook till golden brown, then turn over.

5. When both sides are browned, add the leftover marinade and dress, Place in a serving dish and add the lettuce.

豚肉のしょうが焼き
GINGER PORK

材料（2人分）

豚ロース肉（しょうが焼き用）
·····························200g

しょうが···················· 大1かけ

A | しょうゆ··· ··· 大さじ2 (30ml)
  | 酒·········· 大さじ1 (15ml)
  | みりん········ 大さじ1 (15ml)

サラダ油········ 大さじ½ (7.5ml)
トマト··························適宜

作り方

Aのしょうゆ、酒、みりんを合わせてつけ汁を作り、しょうがをたっぷりすりおろして加える。あとは左と同様に豚肉の下ごしらえをして焼く。器に盛り、トマトのくし形切りを添える。

Ingredients (2 servings)

200g pork loin
  (cut for ginger pork)
1 piece ginger, large

A | 2 tbsp (30ml) soy sauce
  | 1 tbsp (15ml) sake
  | 1 tbsp (15ml) mirin (sweet sake)

½ tbsp (7.5ml) salad oil
Tomatoes, as needed

Directions

Mix the ingredients in A and add a heaping amount of ground ginger. Follow the steps on the left, marinate and cook. Place in a serving dish and add quartered tomatoes.

豚肉のみそ漬け焼き
MISO GRILLED PORK

焼きむらができないようにみそは均一に塗って、あとはオーブントースターにおまかせ。
For the meat to be uniformly cooked apply miso paste evenly, and let the oven toaster do the rest.

357 kcal
1人分
One serving

材料（2人分）

豚ロース肉（とんかつ用）……… 2枚

A｜みそ………… 大さじ3（45ml）
　｜酒 …………… 大さじ1（15ml）
　｜みりん………… 大さじ1（15ml）

サラダ油…………………………少々
グリーンアスパラガス………… 適宜

Ingredients (2 servings)

2 pieces pork loin (for cutlet)

A｜3 tbsp (45ml) miso
　｜1 tbsp (15ml) sake
　｜1 tbsp (15ml) mirin (sweet sake)

Salad oil, to your taste
Green asparagus, as needed

作り方

1. 豚肉は筋切りをして、肉たたき（めん棒でも）で全体を軽くたたいたあと、形を元に戻す。

2. Aのみそ、酒、みりんを合わせてなめらかにまぜ、豚肉の両面にまんべんなく塗って5分おく。

3. オーブントースターをあたためておき、受け皿に軽くしわを寄せたアルミホイルを敷いて、薄くサラダ油を塗る。豚肉をのせて12〜13分焼いて火を通す。アスパラも焼く。

4. それぞれ食べやすく切って、器に盛り合わせる。

Directions

1. Make incisions in the pork meat and pound it (you can use a roller). After lightly pounding all of it, form back into its original shape.

2. Mix all the ingredients in A gently and apply on both sides of the pork meat. Let it sit for 5 minutes.

3. Pre-heat the oven toaster. On a tray, place a layer of wrinkled aluminum foil and coat with salad oil. Place the pork meat on top and cook thoroughly for 12 to 13 minutes. Cook the asparagus too.

4. Cut each into bite-size pieces and place in a serving dish.

肉の焼き縮みを防ぐために、赤身と脂身の間に縦に包丁の先を入れ、1cm長さの切り込みを数カ所入れて筋を切ります。こうして筋を切ることを筋切りといいます。

To prevent the pork from shrinking, make several 1cm long incisions through the lean and the fat. Cutting the muscle parts in this way is called muscle cutting (suji-giri).

肉のおかず・ Meat Dishes

🔍 クッキングメモ

みそと豚肉は相性がよい

豚ロース肉（とんかつ用）は肉質がきめがこまかくてやわらかいのが特徴です。まわりについている脂肪にうまみや風味があるので、その持ち味を生かした和風の味つけにして焼き上げるとおいしさもパワーアップします。

🔍 COOKING MEMO

Pork is well-matched with miso.

Pork loin (for cutlet) meat has a fine texture and is tender. The savory flavor and the umami of the meat fat is best when cooked with well-matched Japanese seasoning.

豚の角煮
JAPANESE-STYLE BRAISED PORK

下ごしらえをしたら、あとはなべまかせ。
After you prepare everything, you can leave the rest to the pot.

816 kcal
1人分
One serving

材料（2人分）

豚バラ肉（かたまり）………… 600g
しょうが ………………………… 1かけ
ねぎ（青い部分）……………… 10cm

A 酒 ……………1 カップ（200ml）
　 水 ………………½カップ（100ml）
　 砂糖 ………… 大さじ1（15ml）
　 しょうゆ ……… 大さじ3（45ml）
　 みりん ………… 大さじ4（60ml）

青梗菜 ……………………… 大½株
ねりがらし …………………… 適宜

作り方

1. 豚肉は5〜6cm角に切る。しょうがは皮つきのまま2〜3mm厚さに切る。

2. フライパンを熱して豚肉を入れ、強火で転がしながら表面にこんがりと焼き色をつける。

3. なべに豚肉、ねぎ、しょうが、たっぷりの水を入れて強火にかけ、煮立ったら中火で1時間30分ゆでる。

4. 豚肉に竹ぐしを刺してみてすっと通るくらいやわらかくなったら、火を止める。

5. ふたをして一晩おく。冷めると豚肉から出た脂が浮いて、白く固まってくる。

6. なべから豚肉をとり出し、ぬるま湯で肉のまわりの脂を洗い落とす。

7. フライパンにAを合わせ、煮立ったら豚肉を入れる。再び煮立ったら弱火にして落としぶたをする。

8. ときどき上下を入れかえながら、ほとんど汁けがなくなるまで30〜40分煮る。

9. 青梗菜を熱湯でゆでて冷水にとり、水けをしぼって食べやすく切る。豚肉とともに盛り、からしを添える。

Ingredients (2 servings)

600g pork belly (chunks)
1 piece ginger
10cm naganegi onion (green end)

A | 1 cup (200ml) sake
½ cup (100ml) water
1 tbsp (15ml) sugar
3 tbsp (45ml) soy sauce
4 tbsp (60ml) mirin (sweet sake)

½ large bok-choy bunch
Karashi paste (Japanese mustard), as needed

Directions

1. Cut the pork into 5 to 6cm cubes. With the skin on, cut the ginger into 2 to 3mm slices.

2. Heat a frying pan to high and sear the pork on all the sides while moving it around.

3. Put the pork, naganegi onion, and ginger in a pot and fill with water. Leave it over high till it starts boiling. Then, turn to medium and boil for an hour and a half.

4. If the pork is tender enough and you are able to easily stick a bamboo skewer through it, turn the heat off.

5. Cover it and leave overnight. When it cools, the fat will float and be hard and white.

6. Remove the pork from the pot and rinse the fat off the pork with lukewarm water.

7. Put A into a frying pan. When it comes to a boil, add the pork. Once it starts to boil again, turn the heat to low and place a drop lid.

8. Occasionally flipping over the pork, simmer for 30 to 40 minutes till most of the liquid has been cooked out.

9. Boil the bok-choy and soak in cold water. Squeeze out excess moisture and cut into bite-size pieces. Serve with pork meat and season with Japanese mustard.

竹ぐしが
すっと
通ったら OK

If the stick is easily poked through, then it is ready.

● クッキングメモ

本格メニューも作ってみると簡単

豚肉の表面を焼いてうまみを閉じ込めてから下ゆでし、一晩おいて余分な脂を抜きます。ほとんど手をかけるところはないけれど、脂を洗い落として煮上げると、すごーく手をかけた感じに見えるうれしいメニューです。

● COOKING MEMO

You'll see how simple it really is!

Sear the pork meat to seal in the umami flavors, boil in water, leave overnight, and then remove the excess fat. This is a dish that doesn't require much work, but if you rinse off the excess fat then braise, it turns out very well and seems as though a lot of time was spent on it.

大根と豚バラ肉の煮物

BRAISED PORK BELLY AND DAIKON RADISH

豚バラ肉のうまみが大根にしみただしいらずの煮物です。
A simmered dish in which the umami flavors of pork belly are soaked into daikon radish.

559 kcal
1人分
One serving

材料 (2人分)

大根 ……………………………500g
豚バラ肉 (かたまり) …………250g

A 酒 ……………… ¼ カップ (50ml)
　 水 ……………2 カップ (400ml)
　 砂糖 ……………大さじ½ (7.5ml)
　 しょうゆ …… 大さじ 1.5 (22.5ml)

グリーンアスパラガス ………… 4本

作り方

1. 大根は乱切りにする。大きさをそろ
えて切っておくと火の通りが均一に
なる。

2. 豚肉は赤身と脂身が層になるように
大きさをそろえて1.5cm厚さに切る。

3. フライパンを熱して豚肉をこんがり
と焼きつけるように炒める。余分な
脂をふきとり、Aの煮汁を加える。

4. 煮立ったら中火にしてアクをとる。大
根を加えて20〜25分煮る。器に盛
り、ゆでたアスパラを添える。

🔍 クッキングメモ

**葉を切り落として
水分の蒸発を防ぐ**

大根はビタミンCが豊富で、葉はほか
の青菜に負けないほどの栄養がたっぷ
り含まれています。できれば葉つきの
ものを購入して大いに活用を。ただし
葉つきのものは、葉や茎から水分が
蒸発するので、買ってきたらすぐにつ
け根から葉を切り離して別々に保存し
ます。

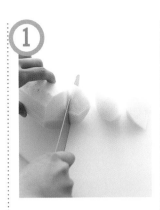

Ingredients (2 servings)

500g daikon radish
250g pork belly (chunks)

A ¼ cup (50ml) sake
　 2 cups (400ml) water
　 ½ tbsp (7.5ml) sugar
　 1.5 tbsp (22.5ml) soy sauce

4 green asparagus stalks

Directions

1. Cut the daikon radish into uniform chunks.
If you keep the sizes all the same, it is
easier for it to cook evenly.

2. Cut the pork into 1.5cm thick slices with
both the fat and the lean attached.

3. Heat the frying pan and sear the pork.
Wipe off the excess fat and add the A
soup broth.

4. After it simmers, turn the heat down to
medium and remove the scum. Add the
daikon radish and simmer for 20 to
25 minutes. Serve with boiled green
asparagus.

 油を入れずに強火で焼きつける
Over high heat, sear without
using oil.

🔍 COOKING MEMO

**Cut off the leaves to prevent
moisture from evaporating.**

Daikon radishes are full of vitamin C, and
the leaves have a lot of nutrients compared
to other greens. Try to purchase daikon
radishes with the leaves on and make use
of them. However, moisture evaporates
from the leaves and stalk, so when you buy
ones with leaves, make sure to cut the
leaves off and store separately.

大根と豚バラ肉の炒め煮・カレー風味

CURRY BRAISED PORK BELLY AND DAIKON RADISH

肉に下味をつける、炒める、とカレー粉のダブル使いで風味をアップ。
Pre-season the meat, sear, and add curry powder to double the flavor.

605 kcal
1人分
One serving

材料（2人分）

大根 ……………………………500g
豚バラ肉（かたまり）…………250g

A ┌ 酒 ……………… 小さじ1 (5ml)
　├ しょうゆ ………… 小さじ1 (5ml)
　└ カレー粉 ………… 小さじ2 (10ml)

サラダ油 ……………… 小さじ1 (5ml)
カレー粉 ……………… 小さじ1 (5ml)

B ┌ 酒 ……………… ¼カップ (50ml)
　├ 水 ……………… 1カップ (200ml)
　├ 砂糖 …………… 小さじ1 (5ml)
　└ しょうゆ ………… 大さじ1 (15ml)

大根の茎 ……………………… 適宜

作り方

1. 豚肉は1.5cm厚さに切り、Aの下味をつけて10分おく。大根は1.5cm厚さの半月切りにする。

2. フライパンにサラダ油を熱し、強火で豚肉をこんがりと焼きつけるように炒める。

3. 大根を加えて炒め合わせ、カレー粉を振り入れてなじむように炒める。

4. Bの酒、水を加え、煮立ったら中火にしてアクをとる。Bの砂糖、しょうゆを加えて落としぶたをし、さらにフライパンのふたをする。

5. ときどき上下を入れかえるようにまぜ、大根がやわらかくなって汁けがほぼなくなるまで25〜30分煮る。

6. 塩ゆでして5cm長さに切った大根の茎とともに盛り合わせる。

Ingredients (2 servings)

500g daikon radish
250g pork belly (chunks)

A | 1 tsp (5ml) sake
　| 1 tsp (5ml) soy sauce
　| 2 tsp (10ml) curry powder

1 tsp (5ml) salad oil
1 tsp (5ml) curry powder

B | ¼ cup (50ml) sake
　| 1 cup (200ml) water
　| 1 tsp (5ml) sugar
　| 1 tbsp (15ml) soy sauce

Daikon radish stem, as needed

Directions

1. Cut the pork into 1.5cm thick pieces, then season and coat with A and leave for 10 minutes. Cut the daikon radish into 1.5cm thick half-moon pieces.

2. Heat the salad oil and sear the pork meat over high.

3. Add the daikon radish and stir fry, then add curry powder to cook in the flavor.

4. Add the sake and water from B. When it starts to boil, turn to medium and remove the scum. Add sugar and soy sauce from B and place a drop lid. Cover the frying pan with another lid.

5. Occasionally mix well, moving the bottom ingredients to the top, and simmer for 25 to 30 minutes until the daikon radish becomes tender and most of the liquid is cooked out.

6. Serve with salt-boiled daikon radish stems cut into 5cm lengths.

POINTER

あらかじめ、酒、しょうゆ、カレー粉を豚肉にしっかりともみ込んでおきます。こうすれば、下味とカレーの香りで肉のうまみがアップします。

Make sure to rub the sake, soy sauce, and curry powder into the pork meat. That way, the pre-seasoning and the curry aroma will boost the umami flavor of the meat.

肉のおかず
Meat Dishes

和風煮込みハンバーグ
JAPANESE-STYLE HAMBURGER

玉ねぎは生のまま加えてふんわりジューシーに。
Add raw onions to keep it fluffy and juicy.

436 kcal
1人分
One serving

材料（2人分）

合いびき肉 ······················· 200g
ねぎ ······························· 1本
しめじ ····························· 1パック

A｜玉ねぎ ························· ½個
　｜パン粉 ··········· 大さじ3 (45ml)
　｜酒 ··············· 小さじ2 (10ml)
　｜卵 ······················· 小1個
　｜塩 ··························· 少々

サラダ油 ··········· 大さじ½ (7.5ml)

B｜だし ··········· 1¼カップ (250ml)
　｜酒 ············· 大さじ2 (30ml)
　｜しょうゆ ·········· 大さじ1 (15ml)
　｜みりん ·········· 大さじ½ (7.5ml)

C｜かたくり粉 ····· 大さじ½ (7.5ml)
　｜水 ················ 大さじ1 (15ml)

あらびきこしょう ··················· 少々

> 中の空気を抜くのが
> おいしくなるコツ
> Remove the air pockets
> for a better taste.

作り方

1. ねぎは斜め薄切りにする。しめじは石づきを切りとってほぐす。Aの玉ねぎはみじん切りにする。

2. Aのパン粉に酒を振りまぜて生パン粉状にし、ひき肉、ほかのAを合わせて粘りが出るまでよくまぜる。

3. 2等分にし、手のひらで軽くキャッチボールをする。これを3〜4回繰り返して円形に形をととのえる。

4. フライパンにサラダ油を熱して③を入れる。こんがりと焼き色がついたら裏返し、反対側も焼く。

5. Bのだし、酒、しょうゆ、みりんを加え、煮立ったらアクをていねいにとる。

6. しめじ、ねぎを加えて4〜5分煮る。Cの水どきかたくり粉でとろみをつけ、あらびきこしょうを振る。

Ingredients (2 servings)

200g ground beef and pork
1 naganegi onion stalk
1 pack shimeji mushrooms

A｜½ onion
　｜3 tbsp (45ml) bread crumbs
　｜2 tsp (10ml) sake
　｜1 small egg
　｜Salt, to your taste

½ tbsp (7.5ml) salad oil

B｜1 ¼ cups (250ml) soup stock
　｜2 tbsp (30ml) sake
　｜1 tbsp (15ml) soy sauce
　｜½ tbsp (7.5ml) mirin (sweet sake)

C｜½ tbsp (7.5ml) potato starch
　｜1 tbsp (15ml) water

Ground pepper, to your taste

Directions

1. Cut the naganegi onion diagonally in thin slices. Cut off the hard ends of the shimeji mushrooms and separate. Finely dice the onion from A.

2. Sprinkle the sake onto the bread crumbs to make them raw. Combine the ground meat and the rest of the ingredients in A and mix well until sticky.

3. Separate into two, then with the palms of your hands, pound out the air pockets. Repeat this 3 to 4 times and shape to form ovals.

4. Heat the salad oil and put 3 into it. When it turns golden brown, turn over and cook the other side.

5. Add the ingredients in B. When it starts to boil, carefully remove the scum.

6 Add the shimeji mushrooms and naganegi onion and simmer for 4 to 5 minutes. Thicken with the starch water from C, then sprinkle ground pepper.

肉のおかず
Meat Dishes

アスパラの牛肉巻き焼き
GRILLED BEEF-WRAPPED ASPARAGUS

手早くできて見ばえよく、大人にも子どもにも人気のメニュー。
Made quick and easy, it is a favorite with kids and adults alike.

249 kcal
1人分
One serving

材料（2人分）

牛もも薄切り肉 ……………… 200g

グリーンアスパラガス ………… 6本

A | 酒 ……………… 大さじ½（7.5ml）
  | しょうゆ ………… 大さじ1（15ml）
  | みりん ………… 大さじ½（7.5ml）

サラダ油 ………… 大さじ½（7.5ml）

Ingredients (2 servings)

200g thinly sliced beef
6 green asparagus stalks

A | ½ tbsp (7.5ml) sake
  | 1 tbsp (15ml) soy sauce
  | ½ tbsp (7.5ml) mirin (sweet sake)

½ tbsp (7.5ml) salad oil

全体にまんべんなくからめる
Marinate evenly.

作り方

1. Aの酒、しょうゆ、みりんを合わせて牛肉にからめておく。

2. アスパラは根元のかたいところを2〜3cm切り落とし、長さを半分に切って牛肉を巻きつける。

3. フライパンにサラダ油を熱し、牛肉の巻き終わりを下にして入れ、転がしながら全体をこんがりと焼く。

Directions

1. Combine the ingredients in A and put in the beef to marinate.

2. Cut 2 to 3cm off the stalky ends of the asparagus. Cut in half and wrap the beef around it.

3. Heat the salad oil and start with the wrapped ends down. Cook while turning it over.

肉のおかず
Meat Dishes

刺し身
SASHIMI

バランスよく立体的に盛りつけて。数は奇数が基本。

Arrange on a plate in a well-balanced and aesthetic way to enhance the experience. An odd number is the standard.

126 kcal

1人分
One serving

材料（2人分）

刺し身用たい	50g
刺し身用まぐろ	50g
生食用サーモン	50g
◎つま	
大根	適宜
青じそ	4枚
穂じそ	4本
おろしわさび	適宜
しょうゆ	適宜

作り方

1. つまの大根は細いせん切りにして冷水にさらし、パリッとさせて水けをきる。青じそ、穂じそ、おろしわさびを用意する。

2. たいは、左側から包丁をねかせて斜めに刃を入れ、5mm厚さのそぎ切りにする。

3. まぐろは1cm厚さに切る。切るときは、包丁の刃元の方をまぐろの手前側に当てて刃先をおろし、一気に手前に引いて切り、右に少しすべらせて離す。

4. サーモンも③と同様にして7〜8mm厚さに切る。

5. 1人分の器の向こう側に、①の大根の半量を箸でふんわりと置き、先端を軽くねじって形をととのえる。大根の左側に青じそ2枚を敷く。

6. 大根の前にサーモンを3切れ盛る。青じその手前にまぐろを3切れ盛り、その上に2切れを少しずらしてのせる。器の手前にたいをバランスよく1切れずつ重ねるように盛り、穂じそ2本をあしらい、わさびを添える。同様にもう一皿盛り込む。

Ingredients (2 servings)

50g sea bream for sashimi
50g tuna for sashimi
50g sushi-grade salmon
◎ Garnish
Daikon radish, as needed
4 ao-jiso green perilla leaves
4 shiso spike stalks

Grated wasabi, as needed
Soy sauce, as needed

Directions

1. For garnish, cut the daikon radish into thin julienne slices and soak in cold water until they become crisp, then drain and prepare the ao-jiso leaves, shiso spike stalks, and grated wasabi.

2. From the left, slice the sea bream into 5mm slices diagonally (sogigiri style) with the knife on a bias.

3. Cut the tuna into 1cm thin slices. When you are cutting, use the end of the blade and cut by slicing and pulling towards yourself, then tilt to the right and let the blade slide off.

4. Cut the salmon the same as 3 and into 7 to 8mm slices.

5. In a single serving dish, lightly pile and garnish the daikon radish from 1 by lightly twisting it to make a nice form. On the left of the daikon radish, place 2 ao-jiso leaves.

6. In front of the daikon radish, place 3 slices of the salmon. Then in front of the ao-jiso leaves, arrange 3 pieces of tuna, then on top place 2 more slices diagonally. In front of the serving dish, arrange the sea bream to balance out the dish, with 1 slice on top of the next. Serve garnished with 2 shiso spike stalks and the grated wasabi. Repeat the same steps for the other serving.

天ぷら
TEMPURA

揚げたての熱々がいちばんおいしい！
Fresh-off-the-fryer tastes the best!

513 kcal
1人分
One serving

材料（2人分）

えび ……………………………… 4尾
なす ……………………………… 1本
生しいたけ ……………………… 2枚
青じそ …………………………… 4枚
◎衣
　とき卵1個分と冷水を合わせて
　……………………… 1カップ（200ml）
　小麦粉 ……… 1カップ（200ml）

揚げ油 …………………………… 適宜
おろし大根 ……………………… 適宜
おろししょうが ………………… 適宜

◎天つゆ（作りやすい量）
だし ……………… 1カップ（200ml）
しょうゆ ………………… ¼カップ（50ml）
みりん …………………… ¼カップ（50ml）

作り方

1. えびは背わたをとり、最後の一節と
　尾を残して足と殻をむく。尾の先端
　を切り、腹側に3〜4か所切り込み
　を入れ、身をのばす。なすは8mm
　厚さの斜め切り、しいたけは軸を切
　り、笠に切り目を入れる。青じそは
　水けをとる。

2. 衣は、「卵水と小麦粉が同量」が基
　本。卵水をボウルに入れてよくまぜ、
　小麦粉を加えて菜箸で大きく5〜6
　回まぜる。粉が表面に残った状態
　でよい。

3. 揚げ油を170〜180度に熱し、え
　びは尾を持って衣をつけ、余分な
　衣を落として油に入れる。青じそは
　裏面だけに衣をつけて揚げる。なす、
　生しいたけは衣にくぐらせて揚げる。

4. 油の音が軽くなり、衣の回りがカリ
　ッとしてきたら引き上げる。

5. 揚げ台に重ねないように置いて油を
　切る。すぐに器に盛り、おろし大根、
　おろししょうがを添え、天つゆ（材料
　を合わせて一煮立ちさせる）を添え
　る。

Ingredients (2 servings)

4 shrimps
1 eggplant
2 shiitake mushrooms
4 ao-jiso green perilla leaves
◎ Tempura batter
　1 cup (200ml) 1 beaten egg mixed with cold water
　1 cup (200ml) flour
　Frying oil, as needed
　Grated daikon radish, as needed
　Grated ginger, as needed
◎ Ten-tsuyu soup broth (an amount that is easy to make)
1 cup (200ml) soup stock
¼ cup (50ml) soy sauce
¼ cup (50ml) mirin (sweet sake)

Directions

1. De-vein the shrimp and peel, but leave the shell near the tail and also the tail. Cut off the tips of the tail, make 3 to 4 cuts in the side and spread out the shrimp. Cut the eggplants into 8mm oval slices and remove the stems of the shiitake mushrooms. Cut a star on the cap, and pat dry the ao-jiso leaves.

2. For standard tempura batter, use equal parts egg-water and flour. Put the egg-water into a bowl and mix well, then add the flour and stir 5 to 6 times with large chopsticks. It's OK if some flour remains on the surface.

3. Heat the frying oil to between 170 and 180 degrees. Batter the shrimp by holding the tail end. Let the excess batter drip out, then fry. Only fry the back side of the ao-jiso leaves. Batter the eggplant and shiitake mushroom, then fry.

4. When the popping sound decreases and it looks crispy, remove from the oil.

5. Place it on a rack, without stacking, and let the excess oil drain. Quickly serve on a serving dish and add the grated daikon radish, grated ginger, ten-tsuyu soup broth (combine all the ingredients then boil).

えびと三つ葉のかき揚げ

MITSUBA TREFOIL AND SHRIMP TEMPURA

シンプルな素材の組み合わせで、和食ならではの香りと歯ざわりを楽しんで。
Combine simple ingredients together and enjoy the authentic Japanese aromas and crispy textures.

345 kcal

1人分
One serving

材料（2人分）

えび	5尾
三つ葉	1束
しめじ	½パック
小麦粉	大さじ1 (15ml)

A | とき卵½個分と冷水を合わせて
　　　　　　½カップ (100ml)
　| 小麦粉　½カップ (100ml)

揚げ油	適宜
レモン	½個

作り方

1. 三つ葉は3cm長さに切る。しめじは石づきを切りとり、ほぐす。

2. えびは竹ぐしで背わたを抜きとる。殻をむいて尾をとり除き、食べやすく二つ〜三つに切る。

3. えび、三つ葉、しめじを合わせてざっとまぜ、小麦粉を振り入れて全体にまぶす。

4. Aのとき卵と冷水をボウルに移してとき、小麦粉を加えて大きく3〜4回まぜて具を加え、さっくりまぜる。

5. 揚げ油を170〜180度に熱し、たねを木べらですくってフライパンの縁に当て、油にすべり込ませる。

6. まわりがカリッとしてきたら裏返し、カラリと揚げる。油をきって器に盛り、くし形切りのレモンを添える。

一度に揚げるのは
2〜3個が目安
Fry 2 or 3 portions at a time.

Ingredients (2 servings)

5 shrimps
1 bunch mitsuba trefoil
½ pack shimeji mushrooms
1 tbsp (15ml) flour

A | ½ cup (100ml) ½ beaten egg mixed cold water
　| ½ cup (100ml) flour

Frying oil, as needed
½ lemon

粉をまぶすと衣がからみやすい
Dusting with flour helps to bind the batter.

Directions

1. Cut the mitsuba trefoil into 3cm lengths. Cut off the hard ends of the shimeji mushrooms and break up into pieces.

2. De-vein the shrimps with a skewer. Peel the shrimp and cut into 2 or 3 bite-size pieces to make them easy to eat.

3. Mix together the shrimps, mitsuba trefoil and shimeji mushrooms and dust with flour all around.

4. Transfer the beaten egg and cold water mixture in A into a bowl and add the flour. Fold 3 to 4 times, add the ingredients and lightly mix together.

5. Heat the frying oil to between 170 and 180 degrees. Scoop the mixture with a wooden paddle and place on the rim of the frying pan, then let the mixture slide in.

6. When the sides start to get crispy, turn over and finish. Drain the oil and serve on a dish with lemon wedges.

さばのみそ煮
MACKEREL SIMMERED IN MISO

最後にみそを入れて風味よく。煮上がってすぐよりも少しおいたほうが味がなじんで美味。
Round out the flavor at the end with miso. Letting it sit for a bit will blend the flavors.

230 kcal
1人分
One serving

材料（2人分）

さば（二枚におろしたもの）… 半身1枚
しょうが ……………………… 20g
昆布………………… 5cm長さを1枚

A｜酒………………… 大さじ2（30ml）
　｜水…………… ¾カップ（150ml）
　｜砂糖…………… 大さじ2（30ml）
　｜みそ…………… 大さじ2（30ml）

貝割れ菜…………………… 適宜

作り方

1. さばは半分に切って、皮目に十文字に切り目を入れる。しょうがはせん切り、貝割れ菜は根元を切る。

2. フライパンに昆布、Aの酒と水を入れ、煮立ったらさばの皮目を上にして入れ、一煮する。

3. さばのまわりが白っぽくなったら、しょうがを入れる。

4. 再び煮立ったら、弱めの中火にしてアクをとる。Aの砂糖を入れ、落としぶたをして8分煮る。

5. Aのみそを煮汁少々でときのばして加える。ときどき煮汁をスプーンですくってかけ、7分煮る。

6. 煮汁が少なくなったら落としぶたをとり、フライパンを揺すって煮汁をからめる。貝割れ菜を添えて盛る。

🔍 クッキングメモ

おいしさの秘訣はここにある！

みそ煮は青背の魚に適した煮方で、魚の生ぐさみが消え、おいしくなります。また魚を煮始めてまわりが白っぽくなったときにしょうがを入れると、加熱されたタンパク質（くさみの成分）としょうがの成分がよく反応してくさみがとれます。「さばのみそ煮」のおいしいわけは、このダブルの効果のおかげ。赤みそ、淡色みそ、田舎みそなど好みのものでさっそく作ってみて。

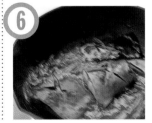

Ingredients (2 servings)

1 mackerel fillet (cut into 2 fillets)
20g ginger
1 piece kobu seaweed (5cm length)

A｜2 tbsp (30ml) sake
　｜¾ cup (150ml) water
　｜2 tbsp (30ml) sugar
　｜2 tbsp (30ml) miso

Daikon radish sprouts, as needed

Directions

1. Cut the mackerel in half and score a cross on the surface of the skin. Julienne the ginger and cut off the ends of the sprouts.

2. Put kobu and A ingredients (water and sake) in a frying pan. When it starts to boil, place the mackerel skin-side up and cook.

3. When the edges of the mackerel start getting white, add the ginger.

4. When it boils again, turn the heat down to medium-low, and remove the scum. Add the sugar from A, put a drop lid on it and simmer for 8 minutes.

5. Add the miso in A by blending it with some of the stewing liquid. Occasionally scoop the stewing liquid and pour it over the fish. Simmer for 7 minutes.

6. When the stewing liquid reduces, take out the drop lid and shake the frying pan from side to side to coat the fish with the stew. Serve garnished with daikon radish sprouts.

🔍 COOKING MEMO

Here's the secret for a delicious fish dish!

Simmering bluish-skinned fish in miso removes the fishy smell for a delicious outcome. When starting to simmer the fish, put the ginger in when the edge of the fish starts to turn white. The ginger will interact with the heated protein (the source of the fishy smell), removing the fishy smell. Doing these two things will make for especially delicious miso-simmered mackerel. You can use your preferred type of miso—red miso, pale miso, or inaka-miso.

魚のおかず Fish Dishes

あじの塩焼き
SALT-GRILLED HORSE MACKEREL

焼く直前に振り塩、化粧塩をして強火の遠火で。
Sprinkle salt on just before cooking. After salting the tail and breast to keep them from burning, cook on high at a good distance from the direct heat.

111 kcal
1人分
One serving

材料（2人分）

あじ ……………………………… 2尾
塩 ………………… 大さじ1（15ml）
大根おろし……………………… 適宜
すだち …………………………… 1個

作り方

1. あじは尾のつけ根から包丁をねかせて入れ、頭に向かって包丁を前後に動かしながらぜいごをそぎとる。

2. えらぶたを広げ、腹側にあるえらのつけ根を切り離し、背側のえらのつけ根も切り離してえらをとり除く。

3. 胸びれの下1cmくらいのところから尾に向かって5〜6cmの切り込みを入れ、内臓をとり除く。

4. 切り口に指を入れて残った内臓と血を手早く洗い流して水けをふく。切り口を下にして腹の中の水けもきる。

5. 皮目に3カ所ずつ切り目を入れる。20cmほど上から塩を振り、尾、ひれに塩をまぶす。反対側も同様に。

6. 焼き網をよく熱してあじをのせ、強火でこんがりと両面を焼く。大根おろしとすだちを添えて器に盛る。

盛りつけるとき表になるほうから
Put the side that you cooked first facing upward when arranging on the dish.

①

②

③

④

⑤

⑥

Ingredients (2 servings)

2 horse mackerels
1 tbsp (15ml) salt
Grated daikon radish, as needed
1 sudachi citrus

Directions

1. Saw off the bony scales, moving from the tail toward the head with the knife lying flat on the side of the fish.

2. Open the gills, cut away the gills closest to the belly, and then cut out the gills closest to the fish's back.

3. Put a 5 to 6cm notch at 1cm from the pectoral fin towards the tail, and then remove the innards.

4. Put your finger inside the notch and remove the remaining innards and blood, wash quickly, and then dry off. Put a notch in the underbelly and remove the water from the belly.

5. Make a notch in 3 places in the skin. Shake salt onto the fish from about 20cm above, covering the tail and fins. Do the same on the other side of the fish.

6. After making sure the grill is well heated, cook the horse mackerel on both sides over high until golden brown. Serve garnished grated daikon radish and sudachi citrus.

324 kcal
1人分
One serving

さんまの塩焼き
SALT-GRILLED SAURY

材料（2人分）

さんま ……………………… 2尾
塩 ……………… 大さじ1（15ml）
大根おろし ………………… 適宜
しょうゆ ……………………… 少々

Ingredients (2 servings)

2 sauries
1 tbsp (15ml) salt
Grated daikon radish, as needed
Soy sauce, to your taste

作り方

1. さんまは半分に切り、内臓をとり除く。血が身にしみると生ぐささが残るので、手早く洗い流して（腹の中も）水けをふく。

2. さんまに塩を振り、よく熱した焼き網にさんまをのせ（盛りつけたとき表になるほうを下にして）、強火でこんがりと両面を焼く。

3. 器に盛り、大根おろしを添えてしょうゆを落とす。

Directions

1. Cut the saury in half and remove the innards. If the blood seeps into the flesh, it will smell, so quickly rinse out the belly of the fish with running water and wipe dry.

2. Shake salt onto the fish and put it on a well-heated grill, first cooking the side that will be served up on the plate. Cook both sides on high until roasted nice and brown.

3. Serve garnished with grated daikon radish with soy sauce poured into it.

いわしの梅煮

IWASHI SARDINES SIMMERED WITH PLUM

梅干しの酸味がさっぱりとおいしくいわしを煮上げます。梅干しの塩分があるのでしょうゆは控えめに。

The acidity of the umeboshi plum simmered with iwashi sardines creates a refreshing treat.
Umeboshi is salty, so use soy sauce sparingly.

323 kcal

1人分
One serving

材料（2人分）

いわし ……………………… 4尾

梅干し ……………………… 2個

A 酒 ………………¼カップ（50ml）
湯 ……………… 1カップ（200ml）
みりん …………… 大さじ1（15ml）
しょうゆ ………… 小さじ2（10ml）

春菊 ……………………………… 適宜

作り方

1. いわしはうろこをとり、胸びれの下に包丁を入れて、頭を切り落とす。

2. 菜箸を切り口から腹の奥までさし込み、菜箸を回すようにねじって内臓を引っぱり出す。

3. 腹の中まで洗ってペーパータオルで水けをふく。さらに切り口を下にして軽く振り、腹の中の水けをきる。

4. フライパンにAの酒、湯、みりん、しょうゆを合わせ、梅干しを二つ～三つにちぎって入れ、強火にかける。

5. 煮汁が煮立ったらいわしを入れる。再び煮立ったら中火にし、落としぶたをして12～13分煮る。

6. 火が通って味がなじんだら、葉先をつんだ春菊を加えて一煮する。

🔍 クッキングメモ

「いわし」はエライ！

いわしは安価なうえに、栄養価が高く、しかも低脂肪、低カロリー。小さいものは骨ごと食べられるので、カルシウムもしっかりとれます。ただし足が早い（鮮度が落ちやすい）ので、買うときは背の青みに光沢があって、うろこがしっかりついている鮮度のよいものを選ぶことがポイント。新鮮さを保つために、買ってきたらすぐ内臓をとって早めの調理を。

Ingredients (2 servings)

4 sardines

2 umeboshi plums

A ¼ cup (50ml) sake
1 cup (200ml) hot water
1 tbsp (15ml) mirin (sweet sake)
2 tsp (10ml) soy sauce

Garland chrysanthemum, as needed

Directions

1. Remove the scales. Insert the knife under the pectoral fin and cut off the head.

2. Insert a large chopstick from the neck deep into the belly. Twist the chopstick and remove the innards like removing a screw.

3. Rinse off the sardine and wipe dry with a paper towel. Point the neck part down and shake a little, removing the water from the belly.

4. Combine the sake, hot water, mirin and soy sauce in A in a frying pan. Break the umeboshi into 2 or 3 pieces and add. Cook on high.

5. Bring to a boil and add the sardines, and then turn to medium when it starts to boil again. Cover with a drop lid and simmer for 12 or 13 minutes.

6. When the fish is fully cooked and the flavor has seeped into the fish, remove the leaves from the garland chrysanthemum, add, and bring to a boil.

🔍 COOKING MEMO

Sardines—more than you think!

Sardines are not only inexpensive, they are also very nutritious. They are low in fat and calories. The smaller ones can be eaten along with the bone, providing a good source of calcium. However, they go bad quickly, so when you buy them, make sure they're fresh—the bluish part of the back should still be shiny, and the scales should be tight. To maintain the freshness, as soon as possible after buying them, remove the innards and cook.

鮭の照り焼き
TERIYAKI SALMON

超簡単フライパン照り焼きです。鮭の切り身を使えば、めんどうな下ごしらえもいりません。
Cooking teriyaki salmon in a frying pan couldn't be easier.
If you use prepared fillets, you don't have to worry about the troublesome preparation.

192 kcal
1人分
One serving

材料（2人分）

生鮭（切り身）···················· 2切れ

A | しょうゆ······ 大さじ1.5 (22.5ml)
　 | 酒················· 小さじ2 (10ml)
　 | みりん··········· 小さじ2 (10ml)

サラダ油··························· 適宜
ねぎ······························· 1本

作り方

1. Aのしょうゆ、酒、みりんを合わせ、鮭にからめて10～15分おく。

2. 鮭をとり出して、ペーパータオルで汁けをふきとる。

3. ねぎは3～4cm長さに切る。フライパンにサラダ油少々を熱し、ねぎをこんがりと焼いて、とり出す。

4. フライパンをきれいにふいて、サラダ油大さじ½ (7.5ml)を熱して鮭を焼く。

5. こんがりと焼き色がついたら裏返し、反対側にもこんがりと焼き色をつけ、弱めの中火にして2～3分焼く。

6. 残ったつけ汁を入れて煮詰め、フライパンを揺すって全体に照りよくからめる。器に盛り、ねぎを添える。

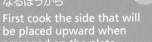

盛りつけたとき上になるほうから
First cook the side that will be placed upward when arranged on the plate.

途中上下を返して味をなじませる
Turn the fillets over to make sure both sides get equally marinated.

Ingredients (2 servings)

2 raw salmon fillets

A | 1.5 tbsp (22.5ml) soy sauce
　 | 2 tsp (10ml) sake
　 | 2 tsp (10ml) mirin (sweet sake)

Salad oil, as needed
1 naganegi onion

Directions

1. Mix the soy sauce, sake and mirin from A, and marinate the fillets for 10 to 15 minutes.

2. Remove the fillets and use a paper towel to wipe the fillets dry.

3. Cut the naganegi onion into 3 to 4cm lengths. Heat a little salad oil in a frying pan, brown the naganegi onions, then remove.

4. Wipe the frying pan clean, heat ½ tbsp (7.5ml) of salad oil, and fry the fillets.

5. When golden brown, turn over, and cook the other side until golden brown. Turn to medium low and cook for 2 to 3 more minutes.

6. Put in the remaining marinating sauce, and move the frying pan over the heat until the sauce covers the entire fish. Serve garnished with the naganegi onions.

ほぼ火が通ったらつけ汁を入れる
Add the marinating sauce when the fillets are mostly cooked through.

鮭の南蛮漬け

SALMON NANBAN-ZUKE
(SALMON MARINATED IN SPICY SOUR SAUCE)

野菜の甘みが酸味をやわらげます。
The natural sweetness of the vegetables softens the tartness.

191 kcal
1人分
One serving

Ingredients (2 servings)

2 salted salmon fillets
½ naganegi onion
1 piece ginger
½ yellow bell pepper

A | 1 red hot pepper
½ cup (100ml) vinegar
1 tsp (5ml) salt
1 tbsp (15ml) sugar
1 tsp (5ml) soy sauce

Frying oil, as needed

Directions

1. Cut the naganegi onion at an angle into thin pieces. Cut the ginger into slices, cut the yellow bell pepper into thin slices and slice the salmon into bite-size, thin diagonal pieces.

2. Soak the red pepper in lukewarm water until soft. Remove the seeds, and then cut into thin pieces. Combine with rest of the A ingredients, add the vegetables and mix.

3. Heat oil in a frying pan to between 170 and 180 degrees, and fry the salmon golden brown. Pour off the oil and, while still hot, add 2 (nanban sauce) and let it seep into the salmon.

材料（2人分）

甘塩鮭（切り身）‥‥‥‥‥‥2切れ
ねぎ‥‥‥‥‥‥‥‥‥‥‥‥½本
しょうが‥‥‥‥‥‥‥‥‥‥1かけ
黄ピーマン‥‥‥‥‥‥‥‥‥½個

A | 赤とうがらし‥‥‥‥‥‥1本
酢‥‥‥‥‥½カップ（100ml）
塩‥‥‥‥‥‥小さじ1（5ml）
砂糖‥‥‥‥大さじ1（15ml）
しょうゆ‥‥‥小さじ1（5ml）

揚げ油‥‥‥‥‥‥‥‥‥‥‥適宜

作り方

1. ねぎは斜め薄切り、しょうがはせん切り、黄ピーマンは細切りにする。鮭は一口大のそぎ切りにする。

2. 赤とうがらしはぬるま湯でもどして種をとり、小口切りにする。ほかのAを合わせ、野菜を加えてまぜる。

3. 揚げ油を170〜180度に熱して鮭をカラリと揚げる。油をきり、熱いうちに②（南蛮酢）につけて味をなじませる。

鮭を揚げる前に用意しておく
Prepare this before cooking the salmon.

かじきのから揚げ
DEEP-FRIED SWORDFISH

くせのないかじきの切り身を使えば、下ごしらえがいらないので簡単。
Using swordfish fillets without strong flavors makes preparation easy.

174 kcal
1人分
One serving

Ingredients (2 servings)

2 swordfish fillets

A | 1 tbsp (15ml) soy sauce
½ tbsp (7.5ml) mirin (sweet sake)
1 tsp (5ml) ginger juice

Potato starch, as needed
Frying oil, as needed
Parsley, to your taste

Directions

1. Slice the swordfish into thin diagonal pieces, and marinate in A (soy sauce, mirin, and ginger juice) for 10 to 15 minutes.

2. Wipe off the swordfish with a paper towel, sprinkle on starch, and then knock off the excess flour.

3. Heat frying oil to between 170 and 180 degrees, and fry the swordfish to a golden brown. Pour off the oil, then serve garnished with parsley.

魚のおかず
Fish Dishes

材料（2人分）

かじき（切り身）・・・・・・・・・・・・ 2切れ

A | しょうゆ ・・・・・・ 大さじ1 (15ml)
みりん ・・・・・・・大さじ½ (7.5ml)
しょうが汁・・・・・・ 小さじ1 (5ml)

かたくり粉・・・・・・・・・・・・・・・・・適宜
揚げ油・・・・・・・・・・・・・・・・・・・・適宜
パセリ・・・・・・・・・・・・・・・・・・・・・少々

作り方

1. かじきは一口大のそぎ切りにし、Aのしょうゆ、みりん、しょうが汁をからめて10〜15分おく。

2. かじきの汁けをペーパータオルでふきとり、かたくり粉をまぶして余分な粉をはたき落とす。

3. 揚げ油を170〜180度に熱して、かじきをカラリと揚げる。油をきって器に盛り、パセリを添える。

粉をつけるのは
揚げる直前に

Sprinkle on the starch right before frying.

さわらのみそ漬け焼き

GRILLED MISO-MARINATED SPANISH MACKEREL

ラップを利用すれば、魚のみそ漬けが手軽にできます。
Using plastic wrap makes for easy preparation of miso-marinated Spanish mackerel.

206 kcal
1人分
One serving

Ingredients (2 servings)

2 Spanish mackerel fillets
 *Japanese Spanish mackerel

A | 2 tbsp (30ml) miso
 | 1 tbsp (15ml) mirin (sweet sake)
 | ½ tbsp (7.5ml) sake
 | 1 tsp (5ml) ginger juice

2 ginger stems

Directions

1. Combine the miso, mirin, sake and ginger juice in A and stir until smooth.

2. Spread out the plastic wrap, and spread 1 (miso doko paste) on half of it. Put the Spanish mackerel on it.

3. Apply the rest of the miso paste to the Spanish mackerel. Wrap it in the plastic wrap and lightly press it. Cool in the refrigerator for 20 to 30 minutes.

4. Roughly scrape off the miso paste, and put on the grate of a baking sheet. Cook for 12 or 13 minutes in a pre-heated oven. Serve garnished with ginger stems.

材料（2人分）

さわら（切り身）………… 2切れ

A｜みそ ………… 大さじ2（30ml）
　｜みりん……… 大さじ1（15ml）
　｜酒………… 大さじ½（7.5ml）
　｜しょうが汁…… 小さじ1（5ml）

はじかみ………………………2本

作り方

1. Aのみそ、みりん、酒、しょうが汁を合わせ、なめらかにときのばしておく。

2. ラップを広げて①（みそ床）の半量を塗り広げ、さわらをのせる。

3. 残りのみそ床をさわらに塗り、ラップで包んで軽く押さえてなじませる。冷蔵庫に入れて20〜30分おく。

4. みそをざっと落として天板の網にのせ、あたためたオーブンで12〜13分焼く。器に盛り、はじかみを添える。

ぶりの照り焼き
YELLOWTAIL TERIYAKI

オーブントースターでできます。
You can prepare it on an oven toaster.

229 kcal
1人分
One serving

Ingredients (2 servings)

2 yellowtail fillets

A | ½ tbsp (7.5ml) sake
1 tbsp (15ml) soy sauce
½ tbsp (7.5ml) mirin (sweet sake)

2 radish

Directions

1. Mix the sake, soy sauce and mirin in A to make a marinating sauce. Put in the yellowtail and marinate for 15 to 20 minutes. Turn it over halfway through cooking so that the flavor is absorbed evenly.

2. Spread a sheet of wrinkled aluminum foil on a plate, and place the yellowtail after wiping it dry. Cook in a preheated oven toaster for 7 or 8 minutes.

3. When it is almost cooked through, apply the remaining marinade, and cook a little more until dry. Repeat this 2 or 3 times.

4. Serve garnished with radish cut in half.

材料 (2人分)

ぶり (切り身) ……………… 2切れ

A | 酒 ………… 大さじ½ (7.5ml)
しょうゆ ……… 大さじ1 (15ml)
みりん ……… 大さじ½ (7.5ml)

ラディシュ ………………… 2個

作り方

1. Aの酒、しょうゆ、みりんを合わせてつけ汁を作る。ぶりを入れて15〜20分おく。均一に味がしみるように途中で上下を返す。

2. 受け皿に軽くしわを寄せたアルミホイルを敷き、汁けをふきとったぶりをのせて、あたためておいたオーブントースターで7〜8分焼く。

3. ほぼ火が通ったら、残ったつけ汁を塗って、乾かす程度に焼く。これを2〜3回繰り返す。

4. 器に盛り、半分に切ったラディシュを添える。

POINTER!

つけ汁をスプーンですくって表面に塗り、乾かす程度に焼きます。これを2〜3回繰り返すと照りよく仕上がります。

Use a spoon to coat the surface, and then cook until dry. Repeating this 2 to 3 times will result in a nice finish.

金目だいの煮つけ

SIMMERED KINMEDAI (SIMMERED ALFONSINO)

金目だいは脂が乗っているわりにはさっぱりとした味わいなので、シンプル調理でさらにおいしく。
Although kinmedai is plump and fatty, it has a refreshing taste, making it a delicious and easy-to-cook fish.

191 kcal
1人分
One serving

材料 (2人分)

金目だい (切り身) ⋯⋯⋯⋯⋯ 2切れ

しょうが ⋯⋯⋯⋯⋯⋯⋯⋯⋯ 1かけ

A ┃ 酒 ⋯⋯⋯⋯⋯⋯ ¼カップ (50ml)
　┃ 水 ⋯⋯⋯⋯⋯⋯ 1カップ (200ml)
　┃ みりん ⋯⋯⋯⋯⋯ 大さじ1 (15ml)
　┃ しょうゆ ⋯⋯⋯⋯ 大さじ2 (30ml)

クレソン ⋯⋯⋯⋯⋯⋯⋯⋯⋯ 適宜

> **魚は煮汁が煮立ってから入れる**
> Put in the fish after the broth starts to boil. →

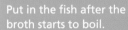

作り方

1. 金目だいは皮目に十文字に切り目を入れる。しょうがはせん切りにする。

2. フライパンにAの酒、水、みりん、しょうゆを合わせて煮立ったら、金目だいの皮目を上にして入れる。

3. 金目だいのまわりが白っぽくなったら、しょうがを入れる。

4. 落としぶたをし、中火で14〜15分煮る。ときどき煮汁をスプーンですくってかけ、均一に味をなじませる。

5. 全体に味がなじんだら、クレソンを加えて一煮する。

🔍 クッキングメモ

これさえわかれば簡単!

煮汁の温度が低いと生ぐさくなります。煮汁が煮立ってから魚を入れるのが、おいしく作るコツ。途中でひっくり返したりすると身がくずれてしまうので、落としぶたをして煮汁が全体に回るようにします。金目だいは煮つけのほかに、蒸し物、なべ物、から揚げ、みそ漬けなどにしても。

Ingredients (2 servings)

2 kinmedai fillets
1 piece ginger

A ┃ ¼ cup (50ml) sake
　┃ 1 cup (200ml) water
　┃ 1 tbsp (15ml) mirin (sweet sake)
　┃ 2 tbsp (30ml) soy sauce

Watercress, as needed

Directions

1. Cut crosses into the skin of the kinmedai. Julienne the ginger.

2. Combine the sake, water, mirin and soy sauce in A into a frying pan and bring to a boil. Put in the kinmedai with the skin side up.

3. When the edge of the kinmedai starts to turn white, put in the ginger.

4. Put in a drop lid, and then simmer on medium heat for 14 or 15 minutes. Occasionally use a spoon to scoop the broth over the entire fish for an even flavor.

5. When the soup has seeped into the fish, add the watercress and bring to a boil.

> ↖ **しょうがを入れてくさみをとる**
> The ginger will remove the fishy smell.

🔍 COOKING MEMO

Here's something that will make it easy!

If the temperature of the broth is low, you'll get a fishy smell. Make sure the broth is boiling before putting in the fish. That will make it taste delicious. If you turn over the fish before it's done, the fish will break into pieces. So, use a drop lid and make sure the broth covers the entire fish. Kinmedai can also be steamed, used in hot pot dishes, deep-fried, and marinated in miso.

いか大根
SQUID DAIKON RADISH

いかのうまみを大根に移しながらしょうゆ味でこっくりと煮ます。
The umami flavor of the squid spreads to the daikon radish as it cooks in a soy sauce flavoring.

179 kcal
1人分
One serving

材料（2人分）

いか	…………………………	1ぱい
大根	…………………………	600g
昆布	…………………	5cm長さを1枚
A	水 ………………2カップ	(400ml)
	酒 ……………… ¼カップ	(50ml)
	しょうゆ …… 大さじ1.5	(22.5ml)

作り方

1. いかは胴の中に指を入れて足と胴のついているつけ根をはずす。胴を押さえて、足をわたごと引き抜く。

2. わたの薄皮についている黒いひも状の墨袋を破かないように、目の下のところからわたと足を切り離す。

3. 胴の中を流水で洗い流し、指を入れて軟骨をとり除く。足も洗う。

4. 胴はペーパータオルで水けをよくふいて、1.5cm幅の輪切りにする。

5. 目と足の中心にあるからす口（口ばし）を指で押し出してとる。

6. 足先を切りとって吸盤をこそげ、食べやすく2本ずつに切る。

7. 大根は縦半分に切って、2cm厚さの半月切りにする。

8. フライパンに昆布、Aの水、酒、しょうゆを入れて火にかけ、煮立ったらいかを入れる。

9. 再び煮立ったら大根を加えて落としぶたをする。ときどき上下を入れかえるようにまぜて40〜50分煮る。

Ingredients (2 servings)

1 squid
600g daikon radish
1 piece kobu seaweed (5cm length)

A | 2 cups (400ml) water
  | ¼ cup (50ml) sake
  | 1.5 tbsp (22.5ml) soy sauce

Directions

1. Put your finger inside the torso of the body, and remove the tentacles attached to the torso. Holding down the torso, pull out the tentacles whole.

2. Being careful not to cut the thin-skinned ink sacks that look like black string, cut off the tentacles from below the eye.

3. Rinse with running water while putting your finger into the torso and remove the cuttlebone. Wash the tentacles.

4. Wipe off all the water with a paper towel. Cut into rings of 1.5cm width.

5. Push out the beak from between the eyes and the tentacles, and remove it.

6. Cut off the tips of the tentacles, remove the suction cups, and then halve the tentacles with two legs together to make it easier to eat.

7. Cut the radish in half lengthwise and then cut into 2cm thick half-moon pieces.

8. Put the kobu seaweed and A ingredients (water, sake, soy sauce) into a frying pan and heat. When it comes to a boil, put in the squid.

9. When it comes to a boil again, add the daikon radish, and cover with a drop lid. Stirring occasionally to bring the bottom ingredients to the top, simmer for 40 to 50 minutes.

包丁の背を使うと
こそげやすい
Suction cups can be easily removed with the back of a knife.

魚のおかず
Fish Dishes

肉じゃが

NIKUJAGA (BEEF AND POTATOES)

でき上がってすぐより少しおいたほうが味がなじみます。
The flavor will be better if you allow it to sit a moment after it's done.

365 kcal
1人分
One serving

材料（2人分）

じゃがいも ………………3個 (450g)
牛こまぎれ肉 …………………100g
玉ねぎ ……………………… ½個
サラダ油 ………… 大さじ1 (15ml)

A | 酒……………… 大さじ1 (15ml)
　 | 水 ………… ¾カップ (150ml)
　 | 砂糖 …………大さじ½ (7.5ml)
　 | しょうゆ ………大さじ1 (15ml)

作り方

1. じゃがいもは大きめの一口大に切り、水にさらして水けをきる。

2. 玉ねぎは縦半分のものを2枚くらいずつにはがして、7～8mm幅のくし形切りにする。

3. サラダ油を熱し、じゃがいもを炒めて表面が透き通ってきたら玉ねぎを入れ、油がなじんだら牛肉を加える。

4. 肉の色が変わり始めたら、Aの酒を振り入れて水を加え、強火にする。

5. 煮立ったら中火にしてアクをていねいにとり、砂糖、しょうゆの順に加えてひとまぜする。

6. 落としぶたをしてさらにフライパンのふたをし、ときどきまぜて汁けがほとんどなくなるまで14～15分煮る。

Ingredients (2 servings)

3 potatoes (450g)
100g thinly sliced beef
½ onion
1 tbsp (15ml) salad oil

A | 1 tbsp (15ml) sake
　 | ¾ cup (150ml) water
　 | ½ tbsp (7.5ml) sugar
　 | 1 tbsp (15ml) soy sauce

Directions

1. Cut the potatoes into bite-size pieces, soak them in water and drain.

2. Peel the first 2 layers off the halved onion and cut it into 7 to 8mm wedges.

3. Heat the salad oil and add the potatoes. When the potato edges become transparent, add the onions. Give the oil time to absorb the flavor, and then add the beef.

4. When the meat begins to change color, sprinkle the sake from A and add the water. Turn the heat to high.

5. When it boils, turn the heat to medium and carefully remove the scum. Add the sugar and soy sauce, in that order, and stir once.

6. Put in a drop lid and cover with the frying pan lid. Simmer and stir occasionally for 14 or 15 minutes until the liquid is almost gone.

じゃがいもがやわらかくなるまで
Until the potatoes are tender.

さつまいものそぼろ煮

SIMMERED SATSUMA SWEET POTATOES WITH GROUND BEEF

酒としょうゆで、おそうざい向きのシンプルな味つけに。
Sake and soy sauce give a simple flavor to this household dish.

571 kcal

1人分
One serving

Ingredients (2 servings)

2 satsuma sweet potatoes (400g)
200g ground beef
1 tbsp (15ml) salad oil
2 tbsp (30ml) sake
1 tbsp (15ml) soy sauce

Directions

1. Leave the skin on the sweet potatoes and slice them into discs 2cm thick. Soak them in water for 10 minutes. Drain well.

2. Heat oil in a frying pan and brown the sweet potato slices. Once the oil has cooked in, add the ground beef.

3. When the meat begins to brown, sprinkle the sake and pour in 1 cup (200ml) of hot water.

4. Bring to a boil. Turn the heat to medium-low, and remove the scum. Add the soy sauce and cover with a drop lid. Stir occasionally. Simmer until the sweet potatoes are tender and the liquid is almost gone.

POINTER

ひき肉を入れるタイミングはさつまいもの両面を香ばしく焼きつけてから。酒と湯は、ひき肉の色が変わり始めたら入れて、肉のうまみをじゅうぶんに引き出します。

Add the ground beef when both sides of the sweet potatoes are browned. Adding the sake and hot water when the meat has just begun to brown will improve the meat's juiciness.

材料（2人分）

さつまいも……………2本(400g)
牛ひき肉…………………200g
サラダ油…………大さじ1(15ml)
酒……………大さじ2(30ml)
しょうゆ…………大さじ1(15ml)

作り方

1. さつまいもは皮つきのまま、2cm厚さの輪切りにし、水に10分ほどさらして水けをよくきる。

2. フライパンにサラダ油を熱して、さつまいもを焼きつけるように炒める。油がなじんでこんがりしてきたら、ひき肉を加えて炒める。

3. 肉の色が変わり始めたら、酒を振り入れて湯1カップ(200ml)を注ぐ。

4. 煮立ったら弱めの中火にしてアクをとり、しょうゆを加えて落としぶたをする。ときどきまぜ、さつまいもがやわらかくなってほとんど汁けがなくなるまで煮る。

さつまいもの甘煮

SWEET STEWED SATSUMA SWEET POTATOES

箸休めにあるとうれしい。
A refreshing side dish.

160 kcal
1人分
One serving

Ingredients (2 servings)

1 satsuma sweet potato (200g)

A | 2 cups (400ml) water
  | 1 tbsp (15ml) sugar

B | Salt, to your taste
  | ½ tbsp (7.5ml) mirin (sweet sake)

Directions

1. Leave the skin on the sweet potatoes and slice them into discs 2cm thick. Soak them in water for 10 minutes. Drain well.

2. Combine water, sugar from A and sweet potatoes in a frying pan. Cover with a drop lid and heat.

3. Bring to a boil. Turn heat to medium and simmer for 10 minutes. When half-cooked, add B and simmer another 7 to 8 minutes until tender.

材料（2人分）

さつまいも ……………1本(200g)

A | 水 ………… 2カップ (400ml)
  | 砂糖 ………… 大さじ1 (15ml)

B | 塩 …………………………… 少々
  | みりん ……… 大さじ½ (7.5ml)

作り方

1. さつまいもは皮つきのまま、2cm厚さの輪切りにし、水に10分ほどさらして、水けをきる。

2. フライパンにAの水、砂糖を合わせて、さつまいもを入れ、落としぶたをして火にかける。

3. 煮立ったら中火にして10分ほど煮る。半煮えくらいでBを加え、さらにやわらかくなるまで7〜8分煮る。

切ったらすぐに
アク抜きする
Soak immediately after cutting to remove scum.

野菜のおかず
Vegetable Dishes

133

里いもの含め煮
STEWED TARO

ほっこりと煮含めて。
Steamy and stewed.

111 kcal

1人分
One serving

Ingredients (2 servings)

10 taro potatoes

A | 2 cups (400ml) soup stock
1 tbsp (15ml) sugar
¼ tsp (1.25ml) salt
1 tbsp (15ml) soy sauce

Directions

1. Wash the taro. Use a scrub brush to thoroughly remove dirt.

2. Peel the taro after drying, rub them in plenty of salt to draw out the water and rinse.

3. Put A in a pot and bring to a boil. Add taro and cover with a drop lid. Put on the saucepan lid as well.

4. When it comes to a boil again, turn the heat to medium. Stir occasionally, moving the taro at the bottom to the top to cook it evenly. Simmer 15 to 20 minutes until tender.

POINTER

里いもにたっぷりの塩を振り、両手でこするようにしてもんでぬめりを引き出します。こうすることによって味の含みがよくなります。

Rub plenty of salt on the taro using both hands to draw out the water and remove the sliminess. The flavor will also seep into the taro.

材料（2人分）

里いも······················10個

A | だし··········2カップ（400ml）
砂糖··········大さじ1（15ml）
塩··········小さじ¼（1.25ml）
しょうゆ·······大さじ1（15ml）

作り方

1. 里いもは水で洗って、たわしでこすりながら泥をよく落とす。

2. 乾かしてから皮をむき、たっぷりの塩でもんでぬめりを出し、洗い落とす。

3. なべにAを合わせて火にかけ、煮立ったら里いもを入れて落としぶたをし、さらになべのふたをする。

4. 再び煮立ったら中火にして、ときどき上下を入れかえるようにまぜ、里いもがやわらかくなるまで15〜20分煮る。

里いものみそ田楽
GRILLED MISO TARO

里いもをやわらかく煮て、甘辛いみそをからめるだけのレシピです。
A recipe of boiled taro covered in sweet and salty miso.

240 kcal
1人分
One serving

Ingredients (2 servings)

10 taro potatoes
1 cup (200ml) soup stock

A | 3 tbsp (45ml) miso
3 tbsp (45ml) sugar
1 tbsp (15ml) mirin (sweet sake)

Ground black sesame, to your taste

Directions

1. Slightly cut off the top and bottom parts of the taro. Peel the skin thickly to create a hexagonal shape. Rub in salt and rinse to remove the slimy texture.

2. Put the soup stock and taro in a pot and put in a drop lid. Cover with the saucepan lid and simmer 17 to 18 minutes until tender.

3. Once the taro are cooked tender, turn the heat to high and cook until the liquid is gone. Combine A and mix with the taro. Serve in a bowl and sprinkle with sesame.

材料（2人分）

里いも……………………10個
だし…………1カップ（200ml）

A | みそ………大さじ3（45ml）
砂糖………大さじ3（45ml）
みりん………大さじ1（15ml）

すり黒ごま………………少々

作り方

1. 里いもは上下を少し切り、側面が六面になるように縦に皮を厚くむく。塩でもんでぬめりを洗い落とす。

2. なべにだし、里いもを入れて落としぶたをし、さらになべのふたをしてやわらかくなるまで17〜18分煮る。

3. 里いもが煮えたら強火にして汁けをとばし、合わせたAを加えて全体にからめる。器に盛り、ごまを振る。

六方むきなら煮くずれしにくい
Cutting them into hexagonal shapes prevents them from falling apart while cooking.

ロール白菜

HAKUSAI CABBAGE ROLLS

くったりと煮込んだ白菜の甘みと、肉のうまみがほどよく調和。
The boiled hakusai juices are a perfect match for the meat's juices.

366 kcal
1人分
One serving

材料 (2人分)

白菜······················ 4枚
豚ひき肉·················200g
ねぎ·····················10cm
しょうが·················1かけ

A｜パン粉········ ⅓カップ (約67ml)
　｜酒··············· 大さじ1 (15ml)
　｜卵······················1個
　｜塩····················· 少々

B｜だし··········· 2カップ (400ml)
　｜酒··············· 大さじ2 (30ml)
　｜塩·············· 小さじ½ (2.5ml)
　｜みりん·········· 大さじ1 (15ml)
　｜しょうゆ········ 大さじ1 (15ml)

作り方

1. フライパンに湯を煮立て、白菜を軸のほうから先に入れてさっとゆで、ざるに上げて冷ます。

2. Aのパン粉に酒を振りまぜる。ねぎとしょうがのみじん切り、ひき肉、ほかのAを加えてよくねりまぜる。

3. たねを4等分にして軽くまとめる。白菜を広げて軸のほうにたねをのせ、一巻きする。

4. 白菜の左右を中央に折りたたんで、あとはくるくると巻いていく。これを4個作る。

5. なべに巻き終わりを下にしてきっちり並べ、Bを加えて落としぶたをし、煮立ったら中火で15〜20分煮る。

Ingredients (2 servings)

4 Napa Chinese cabbage leaves (hakusai)
200g ground pork
10cm naganegi onion
1 piece ginger

A｜⅓ cup (about 67ml) bread crumbs
　｜1 tbsp (15ml) sake
　｜1 egg
　｜Salt, to your taste

B｜2 cups (400ml) soup stock
　｜2 tbsp (30ml) sake
　｜½ tsp (2.5ml) salt
　｜1 tbsp (15ml) mirin (sweet sake)
　｜1 tbsp (15ml) soy sauce

Directions

1. Bring water to a boil in a frying pan, add the hakusai stem-first and boil briefly. Place in a strainer and cool.

2. Mix the sake with the bread crumbs. Finely chop the naganegi onion and ginger, and knead them into the ground beef and other A ingredients.

3. Separate the filling into 4 equal portions and lightly shape. Spread out the hakusai leaves, place the filling near the base, and roll once.

4. Fold the leaf inwards from the left and right and roll up. Repeat with remaining 3 leaves.

5. Arrange the 4 rolls at the bottom of a pot, add B and cover with a drop lid. Bring to a boil and turn the heat to medium. Simmer 15 to 20 minutes.

♀ クッキングメモ

おいしい時期を見のがさないで

白菜は一年じゅう出回っていますが、なんといっても甘みが増しておいしいのは晩秋から冬にかけて。白菜は煮物、炒め物、なべ物、煮びたし、即席漬けなど、主菜から副菜まで幅広く使える優秀素材です。

♀ COOKING MEMO

Don't miss the good season

Hakusai is available year-round, but it has a sweeter flavor from late autumn to winter. Hakusai is a widely used ingredient in a variety of dishes ranging from main dishes to side dishes, including stews, stir-fries, hot pots, boiled dishes dipped in sauce, and pickled vegetables.

野菜のおかず Vegetable Dishes

白菜の刻み漬け
PICKLED CHOPPED HAKUSAI

さっぱりといただく即席漬けは、まさに和風の野菜サラダ。ほどよい塩かげんが野菜を引き立てます。
This refreshing pickled dish is a true Japanese-style salad.
A moderate amount of salt improves the vegetables' flavors.

25 kcal
1人分
One serving

材料（2人分）

白菜······················250g
にんじん···················5cm
レモン·····················⅓個
青じそ·····················5枚
塩·····················小さじ1（5ml）

作り方

1. 白菜の葉は一口大、軸はそぎ切りに。にんじんはせん切り、レモンは薄い輪切り、青じそは2cm角に切る。

2. ボウルに野菜を入れ、塩を振ってざっとまぜる。なじんだら、手でもんでしんなりとさせる。

ポリ袋に入れて作ってもOK →
You can also make it in a plastic bag.

Ingredients (2 servings)

250g Napa Chinese cabbage (hakusai)
5cm carrot
⅓ lemon
5 ao-jiso green perilla leaves
1 tsp (5ml) salt

Directions

1. Cut the hakusai leaves into bite-size pieces and slice the stem into long, diagonal pieces. Julienne the carrot, slice the lemon into thin rounds, and dice the ao-jiso into 2cm pieces.

2. Place the vegetables in a bowl and sprinkle with salt and mix. Once blended, knead by hand until tender.

🔍 クッキングメモ

刻み漬けの塩分は2%

刻み漬けは、短時間で漬け上がる即席漬けの一種。新鮮でみずみずしい白菜やキャベツ、きゅうり、なす、大根、かぶなどが適します。塩を振りかけてもみ、軽い重石をして数時間から1日置けば食べごろになります。日持ちをさせる漬け物と異なり、塩分は2%と控えめにし、生野菜の歯ざわりの良さを楽しみましょう。彩りににんじんなどを加えてもよく、風味つけにせん切りのしょうが、みょうが、青じそ、香りと酸味つけにゆずやレモンなどをまぜ合わせると、いっそう味わい深くなります。

🔍 COOKING MEMO

The salt content is 2% for chopped pickles.

Chopped pickles can be made in almost no time at all. Fresh and juicy hakusai, cabbage, cucumbers, eggplant, daikon radishes, and turnips work well. Rub them in salt, and put them under a light weight—they'll be ready to eat within a few hours, or a day later at the latest. Unlike pickles that can be stored longer, the salt in these pickles is reduced to 2%, so you can enjoy the pleasant crunch of raw vegetables. You can add carrots to improve the color and give it flavor by adding thinly cut ginger, myoga ginger, or ao-jiso. To add scent and vinegary flavor variations, mix in yuzu citrus or lemon. These additions will give depth to the flavor of your pickles.

ほうれんそうのおひたし

SOY SAUCE-FLAVORED BOILED SPINACH

色よくゆでてかつおの風味を添えます。
Cook to a nice color and garnish with dried bonito.

41 kcal

1人分
One serving

材料（2人分）

ほうれんそう･･････････････････200g

A | しょうゆ･･････････大さじ1（15ml）
　 | だし　････････････大さじ1（15ml）

B | しょうゆ･･････････大さじ½（7.5ml）
　 | みりん･･････････････大さじ½（7.5ml）
　 | だし　･･･････････････大さじ1（15ml）

削りがつお･･････････････････ 適宜

> **ゆですぎないことが
> コツのコツ**
>
> Be careful not to overcook.

作り方

1. ほうれんそうは根を切り落とし、株の大きいものは十文字の切り込みを入れて、火の通りをよくする。

2. たっぷりの湯を煮立てて、ほうれんそうをかたい根元のほうから先に入れてさっとゆでる。

3. 余熱でゆですぎにならないように、氷水か冷水にとって手早く冷ます。

4. ほうれんそうは水の中で根元をそろえ、根元から葉先へと握るようにして、水けをよくしぼる。

5. Aを合わせてほうれんそうにからめ、軽くしぼって5cm長さに切る。Bであえて盛り、削りがつおをのせる。

🔍 クッキングメモ

季節ごとに素材の味を楽しめる

「おひたし」は実はいろいろな野菜でつくれます。ほうれんそうのほかに小松菜、春菊、三つ葉、菜の花、さやいんげん、グリーンアスパラガスなどでも楽しめます。

Ingredients (2 servings)

200g spinach

A | 1 tbsp (15ml) soy sauce
　 | 1 tbsp (15ml) soup stock

B | ½ tbsp (7.5ml) soy sauce
　 | ½ tbsp (7.5ml) mirin (sweet sake)
　 | 1 tbsp (15ml) soup stock

Shaved dried bonito, as needed

Directions

1. Cut the roots off the spinach. With large bunches, cut a cross into the stump to allow them to cook easier.

2. Bring a pot full of water to a boil, and put the spinach stems, starting at the harder part, then boil briefly.

3. To prevent overcooking, cool quickly with ice or ice water.

4. Bunch together the stems of the spinach in water, and then squeeze with your hands, moving from the stem to the tips to fully wring out the water.

5. Mix the A ingredients together and dress the spinach. Lightly squeeze the spinach in bunches, and cut each bunch into 5cm lengths. Dress with B and serve garnished with dried bonito.

> **急激に冷やすと色鮮やかに**
>
> Sudden cooling helps to make the color nice and bright.

🔍 COOKING MEMO

A great way to enjoy the flavors of the season!

The ohitashi dish can be prepared with various vegetables other than spinach. You can use komatsuna greens, garland chrysanthemum, mitsuba trefoil, rape blossoms, green beans, and green asparagus, among others.

小松菜と油揚げの煮びたし

STEWED KOMATSUNA (JAPANESE MUSTARD SPINACH) AND DEEP FRIED TOFU

かたい茎を先に入れて葉を加えると火の通りが均一になります。
The komatsuna will cook evenly if you put the stalks in first and then the leaves.

84 kcal

1人分
One serving

142

材料 (2人分)

小松菜 …………………………… 200g
油揚げ …………………………… 1枚

A | だし …………… 1カップ (200ml)
　 | 酒 ……………… 大さじ1 (15ml)
　 | みりん ………… 小さじ1 (5ml)
　 | しょうゆ ……… 小さじ1 (5ml)
　 | 塩 …………… 小さじ¼ (1.25ml)

作り方

1. 小松菜は根を切り落とし、株の大き
   いものは十文字の切り込みを入れ
   て、3〜4cm長さに切る。

2. 油揚げは熱湯をかけて油抜きする。
   湯をきって縦半分にし、1cm幅の
   短冊切りにする。

3. Aを合わせ、油揚げを入れる。煮
   立ったら小松菜を入れて2〜3分
   煮て、くったりしたらでき上がり。

Ingredients (2 servings)

200g komatsuna greens
1 slice abura-age (deep fried tofu)

A | 1 cup (200ml) soup stock
　 | 1 tbsp (15ml) sake
　 | 1 tsp (5ml) mirin (sweet sake)
　 | 1 tsp (5ml) soy sauce
　 | ¼ tsp (1.25ml) salt

Directions

1. Trim off the bottom parts of the komatsuna greens and cut a cross into the stumps. Then, cut the komatsuna into 3 to 4cm lengths.

2. Pour hot water on the abura-age to remove the oil. Drain the water. Cut the abura-age in half lengthwise and slice into 1cm wide strips.

3. Mix together A and add the abura-age. Bring to a boil and add the komatsuna. Boil 2 to 3 minutes until tender.

茎を先に入れて葉を加える
Put the komatsuna in stem-first.

ピーマンとじゃこの炒め物

GREEN PEPPER AND YOUNG FISH STIR-FRY

ほのかにじゃこの塩けがきいたさっぱり味の炒め物です。
A refreshing stir-fry with the salty flavor of jako sardines.

89 kcal
1人分
One serving

Ingredients (2 servings)

5 small green peppers
20g dried baby jako sardines
½ tbsp (7.5ml) salad oil

A | 2 tbsp (30ml) sake
  | ½ tsp (2.5ml) sugar
  | Salt, to your taste

Directions

1. Cut open the green peppers at the top part and remove the seeds. Slice into thin strips lengthwise.

2. Place the jako sardines in a strainer and swirl hot water over them. Drain well.

3. Heat the salad oil and sauté the sardines. Add the green peppers. Stir to lightly coat in oil and turn the heat to high. Add A and cook briefly.

少量なので茶こしを使うと便利!

It's a small amount, so a tea strainer works well!

材料

ピーマン ······················· 5個
ちりめんじゃこ ················ 20g
サラダ油 ········· 大さじ½ (7.5ml)

A | 酒 ············· 大さじ2 (30ml)
  | 砂糖 ········ 小さじ½ (2.5ml)
  | 塩 ··························少々

作り方

1. ピーマンはへたを少し切り落として種を除き、縦に細切りにする。

2. じゃこはざるに入れて、熱湯を回しかけ、湯をよくきっておく。

3. サラダ油を熱してじゃこを炒め、ピーマンを加える。油が回ったら強火にし、Aを加えてさっと炒める。

オクラとまぐろのあえ物
MARINATED OKRA AND TUNA

栄養豊富なネバネバ野菜のオクラと刺し身をあえます。
Marinated sashimi with nutritious gooey okra.

Ingredients (2 servings)

1 bag okra (10 pods)
60g tuna (for sashimi)
80g squid (for sashimi)

A | 2 tsp (10ml) soy sauce
   | 2 tsp (10ml) soup stock

Directions

1. Wash the okra and rub with a generous sprinkle of salt. Boil briefly and place in cold water.

2. Drain the okra and cut into small pieces. Cut the tuna and squid into 1cm square pieces.

3. Combine the okra, tuna, and squid. Mix in the soy sauce and soup stock from A.

92 kcal
1人分
One serving

材料（2人分）

オクラ …………… 1袋（10本）
まぐろ（刺し身用）………… 60g
いか（刺し身用）………… 80g

A ┃ しょうゆ ……… 小さじ2(10ml)
  ┃ だし ………… 小さじ2(10ml)

作り方

1. オクラはさっと洗ってたっぷりの塩を振り、手でこすりつける。熱湯でさっとゆでて冷水にとる。

2. オクラは水けをよくきって小口切りにする。まぐろ、いかは1cm角に切る。

3. オクラ、まぐろ、いかを合わせ、Aのしょうゆ、だしを加えてよくまぜる。

産毛がとれて
色鮮やかになる
Remove the hair and make the color bright.

なすの揚げびたし
FRIED EGGPLANT WITH VINEGAR SAUCE

揚げたてをジュッとつけて熱々を。
Enjoy freshly fried, piping hot eggplant.

201 kcal
1人分
One serving

材料（2人分）

なす	5個
ねぎ	10cm
しょうが	1かけ

A | 酢 | 大さじ3（45ml）
| しょうゆ | 大さじ3（45ml）
| 酒 | 大さじ3（45ml）
| 砂糖 | 小さじ2（10ml）
| 赤とうがらし | 1本

揚げ油 …………………………… 適宜

作り方

1. ねぎは小口切り、しょうがはみじん切りにする。

2. Aの酢、しょうゆ、酒、砂糖、赤とうがらしを合わせてつけ汁を作り、ねぎ、しょうがを加える。

3. なすは皮を縞目にむく。

4. なすは縦半分に切る。皮目に浅く切り目を入れて、斜め半分に切る。

5. 揚げ油を170～180度に熱し、なすを薄く色づく程度に揚げる。油をきって熱いうちに②のつけ汁につける。

🔍 クッキングメモ

なすと油は好相性

なすは油との相性がとてもよいので、揚げたり、炒めたりします。煮る場合も揚げてから煮ると色よく仕上がってうまみも増します。揚げびたしにするとコクがあってさっぱりとした口当たりに。焼く場合は強火で。弱火だと水分が流出してうまみも逃げてしまいます。

Ingredients (2 servings)

5 eggplants
10cm naganegi onion
1 piece ginger

A | 3 tbsp (45ml) vinegar
| 3 tbsp (45ml) soy sauce
| 3 tbsp (45ml) sake
| 2 tsp (10ml) sugar
| 1 red hot pepper

Frying oil, as needed

Directions

1. Cut the naganegi onion into small pieces and finely chop the ginger.

2. Mix together the vinegar, soy sauce, sake, sugar and red hot pepper from A to make the sauce. Stir in the naganegi onion and ginger.

3. Peel the eggplants in alternating strips.

4. Cut the eggplants in half lengthwise. Make shallow cuts in the skin side and slice in half diagonally.

5. Heat the frying oil to between 170 and 180 degrees and fry the eggplant until it changes to a lighter color. Drain the oil from it and dip in the sauce you made in 2 while the eggplants are still hot.

← 口当たりがよく、味も含みやすい
Cutting the eggplant this way makes it easy to eat and improves the flavor.

🔍 COOKING MEMO

Eggplant and oil taste great together.

Eggplant is often sautéed or deep-fried because it's very compatible with oil. The flavor and color will be better if you fry it before simmering as well. Fried eggplant with dipping sauce has a deep flavor and a delicious texture. Grill eggplant over high. The water drains out over low heat, and the flavor disappears.

焼きなす
GRILLED EGGPLANT

穴をあける、焼く、皮をむく。3ステップでできます。
Score, grill, and peel for an excellent and popular three-step dish.

49 kcal
1人分
One serving

Ingredients (2 servings)

4 eggplants

A | Grated daikon radish, as needed
Grated ginger, as needed
Shaved dried bonito, as needed

Soy sauce, as needed

Directions

1. Make a shallow cut around the stems and pierce in several places with bamboo skewers.

2. Heat a grill and cook the eggplants side by side over high heat. Grill thoroughly while rolling the eggplants until blackened all around.

3. Place the eggplant in cold water and peel. Drain well and place in a bowl. Garnish with A and top with soy sauce.

材料（2人分）

なす………………………4個

A | 大根おろし……………適宜
おろししょうが…………適宜
削りがつお………………適宜

しょうゆ…………………適宜

作り方

1. なすはへたのまわりにぐるりと切り込みを入れてがくを切りそろえ、数カ所に竹ぐしを刺して穴をあける。

2. 焼き網を熱し、なすを並べて強火で焼く。転がしながら、全体を焦げるくらいによく焼く。

3. なすを冷水にとり、皮をむく。水けをよくきって器に盛り、Aの薬味をのせてしょうゆをかける。

火の通りをよくして破裂を防ぐ

This helps them to cook evenly and prevents the eggplants from breaking open.

なすのみそ炒め

MISO EGGPLANT STIR-FRY

なすはごま油でこんがり炒めてからうまみたっぷりのみそをからめて。
The eggplant is browned in sesame oil and then slathered in miso.

178 kcal
1人分
One serving

Ingredients (2 servings)

5 eggplants
1 red hot pepper

A | ¼ cup (50ml) soup stock
2 tbsp (30ml) sake
2 tbsp (30ml) sugar
2 tbsp (30ml) miso

1 tbsp (15ml) sesame oil

Directions

1. Peel the eggplants in alternating strips and cut into chunks. Seed the red chili pepper and cut into 2 or 3 pieces.

2. Combine the soup stock, sake, sugar, and miso in A.

3. Heat sesame oil in a frying pan and sauté the red chili pepper and eggplant.

4. Once the eggplant is browned, add the sauce from A and cook until the liquid is gone.

🔍 クッキングメモ / COOKING MEMO

とうがらしは辛いだけではない

和食にもよく使う赤とうがらしは、血行をよくする働きがあり、食欲を増進し、消化も助けてくれるスグレモノ。外皮より種のほうが辛いのでふつうは種をとって使いますが、お好みで。辛みは油にとけるので、とうがらしを先に入れてからなすを加えて炒めます。

Red hot peppers are not just spicy
Red hot peppers are an exceptional food that improves blood circulation, increases appetite, and aids in digestion. The seeds are spicier than the shell, so they are usually removed, but it's up to you. Oil lessens the hot flavor, so sauté the peppers first and then add the eggplant.

材料 (2人分)

なす……………………5個
赤とうがらし………………1本

A | だし…………¼ カップ (50ml)
酒…………大さじ2 (30ml)
砂糖…………大さじ2 (30ml)
みそ…………大さじ2 (30ml)

ごま油…………大さじ1 (15ml)

作り方

1. なすは皮を縞目にむいて乱切り、赤とうがらしは種をとり、二つ～三つに切る。

2. Aのだし、酒、砂糖、みそをまぜ合わせておく。

3. フライパンにごま油を熱し、赤とうがらし、なすを入れて炒める。

4. なすがこんがりとしたら、Aの合わせ調味料を加えて、汁けがなくなるまで炒める。

きゅうりの塩漬け
PICKLED AND SALTED CUCUMBER

きゅうりの歯ざわりとみずみずしさを生かすために、レシピはシンプルに。
The recipe is simple and makes use of the cucumber's juiciness and crunch.

Ingredients (2 servings)

4 cucumbers
1 tsp (5ml) salt

Directions

1. Peel the cucumbers in alternating strips and cut in half lengthwise. Cut into thirds.

2. Place the cucumbers in a bowl and mix with salt. Set aside for a short while.

3. When sufficiently flavored, work the cucumbers with your hands until pliable, rinse and squeeze out water.

28 kcal

1人分
One serving

🔍 クッキングメモ / COOKING MEMO

塩は少量でも味を左右する

塩は味つけだけでなく、下ごしらえにも使います。塩化ナトリウムの純度の高い精製塩、うまみのある自然塩などがありますが、この本では一般的な「精製塩」を使っています。自然塩は塩けが控えめなので分量のかげんを。塩は少量でも料理の味を左右するので必ず味見を。

Even a small amount of salt affects the flavor

Salt is used not only for seasoning, but also when preparing. There are many kinds of salt, such as pure sodium chloride refined salt, and flavorful natural salt, but the recipes in this book are made using regular refined salt. Natural salt is less salty, so the amount will differ. Be sure to taste as you go because even a small amount of salt will affect the flavor.

POINTER

きゅうりは皮を縞目にむきます。これなら味が早くしみ込んで口当たりもよく、ところどころ緑の皮が残って彩りもきれいです。

Peel the cucumbers in alternating strips. They will season faster, have a better texture, and the remaining green skin is also decorative.

材料

きゅうり・・・・・・・・・・・・・・・・・・・・4本
塩・・・・・・・・・・・・・・・・・小さじ1 (5ml)

作り方

1. きゅうりは皮を縞目にむいて縦半分に切り、長さを3等分する。

2. ボウルにきゅうりを入れて塩を振りまぜ、しばらくおく。

3. 味がなじんだら、手でもんでしんなりさせ、さっと洗って水けをしぼる。

きゅうりとわかめの酢の物

PICKLED WAKAME SEAWEED AND CUCUMBER

おなじみの酢の物にたこを加えて。
Octopus is added to this familiar pickled dish.

71 kcal

1人分
One serving

Ingredients (2 servings)

1 cucumber
2g cut wakame seaweed (dried)
100g boiled octopus

A | 1 tbsp (15ml) vinegar
1 tbsp (15ml) soup stock
½ tbsp (7.5ml) mirin (sweet sake)
¼ tsp (1.25ml) soy sauce
Salt, to your taste

Directions

1. Peel the cucumbers in alternating strips and cut into small chunks. Leave in salt water with 1 cup of water (200ml) to 1 tsp of salt (5ml) for 5 minutes. When tender, remove and squeeze out the water.

2. Soak the wakame in water to reconstitute it and wring. Slice the octopus into pieces, making diagonal cuts.

3. Combine A and add the cucumbers, wakame, and octopus.

材料（2人分）

きゅうり…………………………1本
カットわかめ（乾燥）……………2g
ゆでだこ……………………… 100g

A｜酢…………… 大さじ1（15ml）
だし………… 大さじ1（15ml）
みりん……… 大さじ½（7.5ml）
しょうゆ… 小さじ¼（1.25ml）
塩……………………………… 少々

作り方

1. きゅうりは皮を縞目にむいて小口切りにする。塩水（水1カップ・200mlに塩小さじ1・5mlの割合）に5分ほどつけて、しんなりしたら水けをしぼる。

2. わかめは水につけてもどし、水けをしぼる。たこはそぎ切りにする。

3. Aを合わせ、きゅうり、わかめ、たこをあえる。

🔍 **クッキングメモ** / COOKING MEMO

酢の物の共通ポイント

酢の物は簡単そうで奥深い料理です。材料は生で使うことが多いので鮮度には注意しましょう。下ごしらえとして、野菜類は塩でもんで水けをしぼる、魚介類は塩でしめたり、酢にくぐらせて、生臭みをとる、なども大切です。また材料は十分に冷まし、食べる直前に合わせ酢とあえます。

Pointers for pickled dishes

Pickles seem easy to make, but it requires a lot of skill to make them taste delicious. Uncooked ingredients are often used, so make sure everything is fresh. When preparing, rub the salt into the vegetables and drain the water. When making pickles with seafood, sprinkling salt over them and dipping them into vinegar will get rid of smells and improve their taste. Be sure to chill the ingredients sufficiently and dress with vinegar immediately before serving.

野菜のおかず
Vegetable Dishes

151

かぼちゃの含め煮
BRAISED PUMPKIN

だしとしょうゆだけで煮含めて、かぼちゃ本来の自然な甘みを味わいます。
The broth contains only soup stock and soy sauce, so you can taste the natural sweetness of the pumpkin.

Ingredients (2 servings)

450g pumpkin

A | 2 cups (400ml) soup stock
  | 1 tbsp (15ml) soy sauce

Directions

1. Remove the pumpkin seeds and pulp with a spoon. Cut off the rind in a few places and cut into 4 to 5cm pieces.

2. Put the soup stock and soy sauce from A into a frying pan. Bring to a boil and add the pumpkin. Cover with a drop lid as well as the frying pan lid and simmer.

3. Bring back to a boil and turn the heat to low. Simmer for about 18 to 20 minutes until the pumpkin is soft.

211 kcal
1人分
One serving

POINTER

カロチンなどの栄養成分が豊富な皮。なるべく使いたいのですが、味が含みにくくなるので、包丁でところどころ削るようにむきます。

The rind is rich in nutrients such as carotene. You want to use as much as possible, but it will not season well if there is too much rind. So, use a kitchen knife to shave off some parts of the rind.

材料（2人分）

かぼちゃ……………………450g

A | だし…………2カップ（400ml）
  | しょうゆ………大さじ1（15ml）

作り方

1. かぼちゃはスプーンで種とわたをくりぬき、ところどころ皮をむいて4〜5cm角に切る。

2. フライパンにAのだし、しょうゆを入れ、煮立ったらかぼちゃを入れて落としぶたをし、さらにフライパンのふたをして煮る。

3. 再び煮立ったら弱火にして、かぼちゃがやわらかくなるまで18〜20分煮る。

たけのこの焼きびたし

ROASTED BAMBOO SHOOT IN A SOY-BASED SPICY SAUCE

たけのこは下ゆでしてから焼くと、水っぽくなりません。
Boiling the bamboo shoot before roasting it helps remove excess moisture.

85 kcal
1人分
One serving

Ingredients (2 servings)

250g boiled bamboo shoot

A | 1 cup (200ml) soup stock
2 tbsp (30ml) soy sauce
2 tbsp (30ml) mirin (sweet sake)
1 red hot pepper

Leafy lettuce, as needed

Directions

1. Slice the bamboo shoot lengthwise into 7 to 8mm thick pieces. Boil the pieces and drain. Finely chop the red pepper after removing the seeds.

2. Combine the ingredients in A to make the sauce. Heat a cooking grill and roast the bamboo shoot pieces over the gas fire. Place them in the sauce as soon as they are roasted.

クッキングメモ / COOKING MEMO

たけのこのポイント

たけのこは食物繊維が多く、胃腸の働きを活発にしてくれます。独特の風味とうまみがあるので、煮物、白あえ、木の芽あえ、酢の物、たけのこごはん、汁の実など、和食にもよく使います。先端はあえ物、汁の実に、まん中は煮物に、下半分は小さく切ってたけのこごはんなどと使い分けても。

Pointer for bamboo shoot

Bamboo shoot is rich in fiber and helps our digestive system. It has a unique flavor and taste and goes well with Japanese cuisine. It is often used in stews, vegetable salad with mashed tofu dressing, bamboo shoot and sansho pepper shoot salad, bamboo shoot vinaigrettes, bamboo shoot rice, and soups. The upper part is suitable for salads and soups, the middle section for stews, and the lower part can be chopped into small pieces and used in bamboo shoot rice.

材料（2人分）

ゆでたけのこ……………… 250g

A | だし…………1 カップ（200ml）
しょうゆ………大さじ2 (30ml)
みりん………大さじ2 (30ml)
赤とうがらし……………1本

サラダ菜………………… 適宜

作り方

1. たけのこは7〜8mm厚さに縦に切り、下ゆでして水けをきる。赤とうがらしは種をとって小口切りにする。

2. Aを合わせてつけ汁を作る。焼き網を熱し、たけのこを焼く。こんがりと焼き色がついたら、つけ汁につける。

野菜のおかず
Vegetable Dishes

153

アスパラのごまあえ

ASPARAGUS DRESSED IN SESAME SEEDS

アスパラを香ばしく焼いてごまたっぷりのあえ衣であえます。
Outstanding flavor of roasted asparagus dressed in a thick sesame dressing.

60 kcal
1人分
One serving

Ingredients (2 servings)

10 green asparagus stalks

A | ½ tbsp (7.5ml) soy sauce
½ tbsp (7.5ml) mirin (sweet sake)
1 tbsp (15ml) soup stock

10g chopped white sesame

Directions

1. Cut off the bottom 1 to 2cm of the asparagus to remove the hard part.

2. Roast the asparagus on a hot cooking grill and cut into 4 to 5cm lengths.

3. Combine the ingredients in A (soy sauce, mirin, and soup stock). Add chopped sesame and the roasted asparagus.

POINTER

転がしながら焼くと、全体に火が通ってきれいな焼き色がつきます。焼き網がなかったら、魚焼きグリル、オーブントースターで。

Moving the asparagus around while roasting will ensure even coloring. If a cooking grill is not available, a fish grill or an oven-toaster will do.

材料（2人分）

グリーンアスパラガス………10本

A | しょうゆ …… 大さじ½ (7.5ml)
みりん………大さじ½ (7.5ml)
だし ………… 大さじ1 (15ml)

切り白ごま…………………10g

作り方

1. アスパラは根元のかたいところを1〜2cm切り落とす。

2. 焼き網を熱してアスパラを焼き、4〜5cm長さに切る。

3. Aのしょうゆ、みりん、だしを合わせる。ごまを加えてよくまぜ、アスパラをあえる。

ねぎとあさりの煮びたし

SIMMERED NAGANEGI ONION AND JAPANESE LITTLENECK CLAM

煮汁をたっぷり張って盛りつけます。
Served with plenty of natural soup stock.

58 kcal
1人分
One serving

Ingredients (2 servings)

2 naganegi onions
80g shelled Japanese littleneck clams

A | 1 cup (200ml) soup stock
2 tbsp (30ml) sake
¼ tsp (1.25ml) salt
½ tsp (2.5ml) soy sauce

Directions

1. Cut diagonally in 1cm lengths.

2. Rinse the clams in salt water with a ratio of 1 cup of water (200ml) to 1 tsp of salt (5ml), and then drain well.

3. Put A in a frying pan and bring to a boil, then add the naganegi onions and bring to a boil again. When the onions become limp, add the clams and cook through.

振り洗いして
ぬめりを落とす
Rinsing the clams removes the sliminess.

材料（2人分）

ねぎ･･････････････････････2本
あさりのむき身･･････････････80g

A｜だし･･････････1カップ(200ml)
酒････････････大さじ2 (30ml)
塩･･･････････小さじ¼ (1.25ml)
しょうゆ･････小さじ½ (2.5ml)

作り方

1. ねぎは1cm幅の斜め切りにする。

2. あさりは塩水（水1カップ・200mlに塩小さじ1・5mlの割合）で振り洗いして、水けをよくきる。

3. フライパンにAを合わせ、煮立ったらねぎを入れて一煮する。しんなりしたら、あさりを加えて火を通す。

野菜のおかず
Vegetable Dishes

わけぎとあさりのぬた

WAKEGI AND JAPANESE LITTLENECK CLAM IN MISO SAUCE

わけぎと相性のいいあさりを、まろやかな酸味の酢で。
Scallions go well with Japanese littleneck clams in a mild vinegar-miso sauce.

123 kcal
1人分
One serving

Ingredients (2 servings)

1 bunch wakegi green onions
80g shelled Japanese littleneck clams
1 tbsp (15ml) sake

A | 3 tbsp (45ml) miso
  | 2 tbsp (30ml) sugar
  | 1.5 tbsp (22.5ml) vinegar

Directions

1. Cut the wakegi in two, parboil till bright green, cool down in cold water and squeeze out excess water. Cut them into 3cm long pieces.

2. Rinse the clams in salty water (see page 155) and drain. Put them in a pot, sprinkling with sake. Cool them down after briefly cooking them at a high temperature.

3. Dress the wakegi and clams in the miso sauce by combining the ingredients in A (miso, sugar, and vinegar).

ゆでるときは根元
から先に入れて
Put the wakegi in roots-first when parboiling.

材料 (2人分)

わけぎ・・・・・・・・・・・・・・・・・・・・・・・・・1束
あさりのむき身・・・・・・・・・・・・・・・80g
酒・・・・・・・・・・・・・・・大さじ1 (15ml)

A | みそ・・・・・・・・・・大さじ3 (45ml)
  | 砂糖・・・・・・・・・大さじ2 (30ml)
  | 酢・・・・・・・大さじ1.5 (22.5ml)

作り方

1. わけぎは半分に切り、熱湯で色よくゆで、冷水にとる。水けをしぼり、3cm長さに切る。

2. あさりは塩水 (p.155) で振り洗いして水けをきる。なべに入れて酒を振り、強火でいりつけて冷ます。

3. Aのみそ、砂糖、酢をよくまぜ合わせ、わけぎ、あさりを加えてあえる。

きのこのかき揚げ

DEEP-FRIED MIXED MUSHROOMS

塩をつけてさっぱりと、きのこの香りを楽しみます。
Salt gives them a nice refreshing flavor and brings out the fragrance of the mushrooms.

325 kcal
1人分
One serving

Ingredients (2 servings)

1 pack shimeji mushrooms
1 pack maitake mushrooms
½ naganegi onion
1 tbsp (15ml) flour

A | ½ cup (100ml) of cold water and
½ beaten egg
½ cup (100ml) flour

Frying oil, as needed
Salt, as needed

Directions

1. Cut off the stems of the shimeji and maitake mushrooms and break apart. Thinly slice the naganegi onion diagonally.

2. Add flour to the mushroom and onion mixture and toss.

3. Put the water and egg in A in a bowl, add flour, and stir roughly 3 or 4 times. Add the mushrooms and onion mixture 2 and stir roughly again.

4. Heat the frying oil to between 170 and 180 degrees. Use a tablespoon to scoop bite-size portions of the mushroom, egg and flour mixture onto the pan, allowing the portions to slide into the frying oil. When the edges turn golden brown, turn the nuggets over and fry them to a nice, even color.

材料（2人分）

しめじ･････････････････1パック
まいたけ ･･････････････1パック
ねぎ････････････････････½本
小麦粉･･････････････大さじ1(15ml)

A | とき卵½個分と冷水を合わせて
････････････½カップ (100ml)
小麦粉 ･･････½カップ (100ml)

揚げ油 ･･････････････････適宜
塩･･･････････････････････適宜

作り方

1. しめじ、まいたけは石づきを切りとり、ほぐす。ねぎは斜め薄切りにする。

2. 材料を合わせて小麦粉を振り入れ、全体にまぶす。

3. Aのとき卵と冷水をボウルに移してよくとき、小麦粉を加えて大きく3〜4回まぜて②を加え、さっくりまぜる。

4. 揚げ油を170〜180度に熱して、たねを大きいスプーンですくって一口大にまとめ、油にすべり込ませる。まわりがカリッとしてきたら裏返し、カラリと色よく揚げる。

POINTER

材料に小麦粉を振り、菜箸でまぜて全体にまぶしておきます。こうしておけば、衣がよくからんで、まとまりやすくなります。

By fully coating the ingredients with flour and stirring with large chopsticks, the batter will stay on easier and the oil will cook in well for nice evenly-cooked nuggets.

大根サラダ

DAIKON RADISH SALAD

大根とラディッシュの和風サラダ。
A Japanese salad with daikon and radish.

91 kcal
1人分
One serving

Ingredients (2 servings)

200g daikon radish
2 radishes

A | 2 tsp (10ml) soy sauce
2 tbsp (30ml) vinegar
Ground pepper, to your taste
1 tbsp (15ml) sesame oil

Shaved dried bonito, as needed

Directions

1. Julienne the daikon radish. Slice the radishes thinly.

2. Soak the daikon radish and the radishes in cold water to make them crisp for 7 to 8 minutes and drain.

3. Make a dressing by combining the soy sauce, vinegar, ground pepper, and sesame oil in A.

4. Place the daikon radish and the radishes in a serving bowl and put dried bonito on top. Pour the dressing immediately before serving.

材料（2人分）

大根　‥‥‥‥‥‥‥‥‥‥‥200g
ラディッシュ‥‥‥‥‥‥‥‥2個

A｜しょうゆ‥‥‥小さじ2（10ml）
酢‥‥‥‥‥‥大さじ2（30ml）
こしょう‥‥‥‥‥‥‥‥少々
ごま油‥‥‥‥大さじ1（15ml）
削りがつお‥‥‥‥‥‥‥‥‥適宜

作り方

1. 大根はせん切りにし、ラディッシュは薄い輪切りにする。

2. 大根とラディッシュは、それぞれ冷水に7〜8分放してパリッとさせ、水けをよくきる。

3. Aのしょうゆ、酢、こしょう、ごま油を合わせてドレッシングを作る。

4. 器に大根とラディッシュを盛り、削りがつおをのせて、食べる直前にドレッシングをかける。

POINTER

大根はざるに上げて水けをきります。さらに大根をふきんで茶巾しぼりのように包んで軽く振ります。

Daikon radish can be drained in a strainer and lightly squeezed in a dish towel.

大根とにんじんの甘酢あえ

DAIKON RADISH AND CARROT IN SWEET-AND-SOUR SAUCE

水けをしっかりしぼって、甘酢の味が薄まらないようにします。
Remove excess water from the vegetables, and you will not dilute the sweet-and-sour vinegar dressing.

Ingredients (2 servings)

250g daikon radish
⅓ small carrot

A | 2 tbsp (30ml) vinegar
⁤ | ¼ tsp (1.25ml) salt
⁤ | ½ tbsp (7.5ml) sugar
⁤ | ½ tbsp (7.5ml) mirin (sweet sake)
⁤ | ½ tbsp (7.5ml) soup stock

Directions

1. Julienne the daikon radish and carrot.

2. Put the desired amount of salt on the daikon radish and carrot, and mix well. When the vegetables soften, rinse and squeeze.

3. Combine the ingredients in A and toss with the vegetables. Let it sit for 5 to 6 minutes.

53 kcal
1人分
One serving

POINTER!

塩をして軽くもみ、しんなりしたら水で洗って水けをよくしぼると、余分な水分が抜けて味のからみもよく、おいしく仕上がります。

Lightly kneading salt into the vegetables, and then rinsing and squeezing them well after they soften will make them taste good.

材料（2人分）

大根······························250g
にんじん························小⅓本
A｜酢·············大さじ2 (30ml)
　｜塩··········小さじ¼ (1.25ml)
　｜砂糖········大さじ½ (7.5ml)
　｜みりん········大さじ½ (7.5ml)
　｜だし··········大さじ½ (7.5ml)

作り方

1. 大根、にんじんはせん切りにする。

2. それぞれに塩少々を振り、全体にまぶす。しんなりしたらさっと洗って水けをよくしぼる。

3. Aを合わせ、大根とにんじんをあえて5〜6分おく。

野菜のおかず
Vegetable Dishes

159

かぶのそぼろあん

TURNIP WITH REFRESHING MEAT SAUCE

かぶを煮た煮汁でそぼろあんを作ります。
Make meat sauce in broth used to boil turnips.

209 kcal
1人分
One serving

材料（2人分）

かぶ	………………………	4個
鶏ひき肉	…………………	150g
A	だし………	1.5 カップ（300ml）
	酒……………	大さじ2（30ml）
	しょうゆ……	大さじ1（15ml）
	砂糖…………	大さじ½（7.5ml）
酒	………………	大さじ1（15ml）
B	かたくり粉……	小さじ2（10ml）
	水……………	小さじ2（10ml）

作り方

1. かぶは横に1cm 厚さに切る。好みで皮をむいても。

2. Aを合わせ、煮立ったらかぶを入れて12〜13分煮る。やわらかくなったら、とり出す。

3. ひき肉に酒を加えてまぜ、②の煮汁に加える。手早くほぐして火を通し、アクをていねいにとる。

4. Bの水どきかたくり粉を加えてとろみをつけ、そぼろあんを作る。器にかぶを盛り、そぼろあんをかける。

かぶのしょうゆ漬け

TURNIP PICKLED IN SOY SAUCE

Ingredients
(2 servings)

4 turnips
150g ground chicken

A | 1.5 cups (300ml) soup stock
   | 2 tbsp (30ml) sake
   | 1 tbsp (15ml) soy sauce
   | ½ tbsp (7.5ml) sugar

1 tbsp (15ml) sake

B | 2 tsp (10ml) potato starch
   | 2 tsp (10ml) water

Directions

1. Cut up the turnips into 1cm thick rounds. They may be pared if preferred.

2. Combine the ingredients in A and bring to a boil. Add the turnips and cook for 12 to 13 minutes. Remove them when cooked through.

3. Add sake to the ground chicken and add it to the broth from 2. Break up the lumps of meat and heat through. Carefully remove the scum from the broth surface.

4. Combine the ingredients in B (the starch and water) and add to the meat sauce to thicken. Place the cooked turnips in a serving dish and pour the meat sauce over them.

ほんの一手間の飾り切りで、味のからみ、食感、見た目もぐっとよくなります。
Go one step further and slice the turnips decoratively to add color, taste, and texture.

35 kcal
1人分
One serving

材料（2人分）

かぶ·····························　小6個
赤とうがらし·······················2本

A | しょうゆ···········大さじ1（15ml）
   | 酒·················小さじ1（5ml）

作り方

1. かぶは茎を1～2cm残して葉を切り落とし、水の中で竹ぐしを使って茎の間の汚れをとり除く。

2. かぶは縦半分に切って切り口を伏せ、端から1～2mm幅の切り込みを入れながら1cm幅で切り離す。

3. Aを合わせて漬け汁を作り、種をとって二つ～三つにちぎった赤とうがらしを加える。

4. かぶを漬け汁に30分ほど漬ける。

Ingredients (2 servings)

6 small turnips
2 red hot peppers

A | 1 tbsp (15ml) soy sauce
   | 1 tsp (5ml) sake

Directions

1. Cut off the turnip leaves, leaving 1 to 2cm of the stems from the top. Using a bamboo skewer, clean out dirt imbedded among the stems in water.

2. Split the turnips lengthwise in half. Turn the cut-side down, make 1 to 2mm incisions and cut each half into 1cm thick pieces.

3. Combine the ingredients in A. Remove the seeds from the red peppers, cut them into 2 or 3 pieces, and add.

4. Pickle the turnips in the mixture for 30 minutes before serving them.

たたきごぼう
CRACKED BURDOCK

ごぼうをたたいて繊維をつぶすと香りが立ちます。
By hitting and cracking burdock, you can break up the fiber
and bring out the flavor.

167 kcal

1人分
One serving

Ingredients (2 servings)

1 large burdock

A | ½ cup (100ml) soup stock
1 tsp (5ml) sugar
Salt, to your taste
1 tsp (5ml) soy sauce

B | 3 tbsp (45ml) chopped white sesame
1 tbsp (15ml) vinegar
2 tsp (10ml) sugar
1 tsp (5ml) soy sauce
Salt, to your taste

Directions

1. Cut the burdock into 12cm long pieces and boil them in hot water with a little vinegar for 7 to 8 minutes. Drain and crack the burdock pieces by pounding them lightly.

2. Cut the burdock pieces into 3 to 4cm lengths and split them by hand into bite-size pieces. Add the seasonings in A and cook till all the moisture is gone.

3. Combine the ingredients in B and add the cooled burdock.

材料（2人分）

ごぼう‥‥‥‥‥‥‥‥‥‥‥大1本

A｜だし‥‥‥‥ ½カップ（100ml）
　砂糖‥‥‥‥‥‥小さじ1（5ml）
　塩‥‥‥‥‥‥‥‥‥‥‥‥少々
　しょうゆ‥‥‥‥ 小さじ1（5ml）

B｜切り白ごま‥‥‥大さじ3（45ml）
　酢‥‥‥‥‥‥‥大さじ1（15ml）
　砂糖‥‥‥‥‥‥小さじ2（10ml）
　しょうゆ‥‥‥‥小さじ1（5ml）
　塩‥‥‥‥‥‥‥‥‥‥‥‥少々

作り方

1. ごぼうは12cm長さに切り、酢少々を加えた湯で7〜8分ゆでて湯をきる。軽くたたいてひびを入れる。

2. 3〜4cm長さに切って手で食べやすい大きさに裂く。Aを合わせてごぼうを入れ、汁けがなくなるまで煮る。

3. Bのごま、酢、砂糖、しょうゆ、塩を合わせ、冷ましたごぼうを加えてあえる。

ひびが入ると味がよくなじむ
Cracking helps them absorb the seasonings.

きんぴらごぼう

KIMPIRA GOBO (STIR-FRIED BURDOCK)

ごぼうはアクが出ないように強火でさっと炒めて表面に火を通して。
It is best to stir-fry the burdock at high heat so that there is no scum.

103 kcal
1人分
One serving

Ingredients (2 servings)

1 small burdock
1 red hot pepper
½ tbsp (7.5ml) sesame oil

A | 2 tbsp (30ml) sake
1 cup (200ml) soup stock
2 tsp (10ml) sugar
¼ tsp (1.25ml) salt
½ tbsp (7.5ml) soy sauce

Directions

1. Scrape off the burdock skin and cut it into long, thin shavings. Put the shavings in water for 15 minutes and drain.

2. Remove seeds from the red pepper and cut it into thinly sliced rings. Heat the sesame oil, and stir-fry the red pepper and the burdock over high heat.

3. When the moisture evaporates and the oil has seeped in, add the seasonings in A. Stir from time to time on medium heat until the moisture is gone.

材料 (2人分)

ごぼう………………………小1本
赤とうがらし………………1本
ごま油…………大さじ½ (7.5ml)

A | 酒…………大さじ2 (30ml)
だし…………1カップ (200ml)
砂糖…………小さじ2 (10ml)
塩…………小さじ¼ (1.25ml)
しょうゆ……大さじ½ (7.5ml)

作り方

1. ごぼうは皮をこそげてささがきにし、水に15分さらして水けをきる。

2. 赤とうがらしは種をとり、小口切りにする。ごま油を熱して強火で赤とうがらし、ごぼうを炒める。

3. 水けがとんで油がなじんだらAを加える。中火にしてときどきまぜ、汁けがなくなるまでいりつける。

水を入れたボウルの上で
Making the shavings over a bowl of water.

野菜のおかず
Vegetable Dishes

れんこんのはさみ揚げ
FRIED LOTUS ROOT WITH FILLING

味、ボリューム、見ばえも充実の一皿。
This is a tasty, filling and attractive dish.

425 kcal
1人分
One serving

材料（2人分）

れんこん	…………………	150g
豚ひき肉	…………………	150g
A	ねぎ …………………	10cm
	しょうが …………………	1かけ
	酒 …………	大さじ1（15ml）
	塩 …………	小さじ¼（1.25ml）
小麦粉	…………………	適宜
かたくり粉	…………………	適宜
揚げ油	…………………	適宜
ライム	…………………	½個
ねりがらし	…………………	少々

作り方

1. れんこんは5mm厚さの輪切りを12枚とる。水に7〜8分さらして水けをふく。

2. Aのねぎ、しょうがはみじん切りにしてひき肉に加え、ほかのAも加えてよくねりまぜ、6等分にする。

3. れんこんに小麦粉を振ってたねをのせ、もう1枚は粉を振ったほうを内側にしてかぶせ、しっかりはさむ。

4. まわりにかたくり粉をまぶして余分な粉をはたき落とし、170〜180度に熱した揚げ油でこんがりと揚げる。

①

②

③

④

れんこんのきんぴら

SPICY SHICHIMI PEPPER AND LOTUS ROOT KIMPIRA

Ingredients
(2 servings)

150g lotus root
150g ground pork

A | 10 cm naganegi onion
1 piece ginger
1 tbsp (15ml) sake
¼ tsp (1.25ml) salt

Flour, as needed
Potato starch, as needed
Frying oil, as needed
½ lime
Hot mustard paste, to your taste

Directions

1. Cut the lotus root into 12 5mm thick slices. Soak the slices in water for 7 to 8 minutes and dry them with a towel.

2. Chop the naganegi onion and ginger from A, and add to the ground pork. Add the ingredients in A, mix well and divide into 6 portions.

3. Take a pair of lotus root pieces and sprinkle flour on one side of each piece. Place a portion of filling on one piece and press the other on top, making sure that the floured sides touch the filling.

4. Coat each set with starch. Shake off the excess starch and fry till brown in oil heated to between 170 and 180 degrees.

強火で一気に。
Lotus root needs to be cooked quickly at high heat.

165 kcal
1人分
One serving

材料（2人分）

れんこん·····················300g
ごま油···············大さじ½（7.5ml）

A | 酒················大さじ2（30ml）
だし············¾カップ（150ml）
みりん··········大さじ½（7.5ml）
しょうゆ··········大さじ1（15ml）

七味とうがらし·····················適宜

作り方

1. れんこんは1〜2mm厚さの輪切りにし、水に10分さらして水けをきる。

2. フライパンにごま油を熱し、強火でれんこんを炒める。水けがとんで油がなじんだらAを加え、中火にしてときどきまぜ、汁けがなくなるまでいりつける。

3. 器に盛り、七味とうがらしを振る。

Ingredients (2 servings)

300g lotus root
½ tbsp (7.5ml) sesame oil

A | 2 tbsp (30ml) sake
¾ cup (150ml) soup stock
½ tbsp (7.5ml) mirin (sweet sake)
1 tbsp (15ml) soy sauce
Shichimi pepper, as needed

Directions

1. Slice the lotus root into 1 to 2mm thick pieces. Soak the pieces in water for 10 minutes and drain.

2. Heat the sesame oil in a frying pan and stir-fry the lotus root at high heat. When the excess moisture is gone, add the ingredients in A and reduce heat to medium. Stir-fry occasionally until all the moisture is gone.

3. Serve with shichimi pepper sprinkled on top.

だし巻き卵
JAPANESE OMELET

口の中でじわっとだしが広がる、ふんわりやさしい食感。
The soup stock flavor fills your mouth as you bite into the fluffy,
soft texture of a Japanese omelet.

196 kcal
1人分
One serving

材料（2人分）

卵		4個
A	だし	½カップ（100ml）
	酒	大さじ1（15ml）
	砂糖	大さじ1（15ml）
	塩	小さじ⅓（約1.7ml）
	しょうゆ	小さじ⅓（約1.7ml）
サラダ油		少々
大根おろし		適宜

作り方

1. 卵を割り入れ、卵白はつまんで切るようにほぐす。泡立てないようにときほぐし、合わせたAを加えてまぜる。

2. 卵焼きなべを熱してサラダ油をなじませ、余分な油はペーパータオルでふきとる。

3. 卵液の¼量を流し入れて、卵焼きなべを回すようにして動かし、卵液を全体に広げる。

4. 半熟状になったら、菜箸で手前から向こうに巻きながら寄せる。

5. あいたところにサラダ油を薄く塗る。

6. 残りの卵液を¼〜⅓量流し入れる。

7. 向こうに寄せた卵を持ち上げて下側にも流し込み、卵焼きなべ全体に広げる。

8. 半熟状になったら表面が乾く前に、向こうから手前に巻く。

9. あいたところに油を塗って卵を向こうに移し、手前にも油を塗って卵液を流し、同様にして焼く。

Ingredients (2 servings)

4 eggs

A | ½ cup (100ml) soup stock
  | 1 tbsp (15ml) sake
  | 1 tbsp (15ml) sugar
  | ⅓ tsp (about 1.7ml) salt
  | ⅓ tsp (about 1.7ml) soy sauce

Salad oil, to your taste
Grated daikon radish, as needed

Directions

1. Break the eggs into a bowl and beat them by running chopsticks through the eggwhite. Be careful not to foam them up. Add to A.

2. Heat an omelet pan and add oil. Remove excess oil with a paper towel.

3. Add ¼ of the egg mixture to the pan and move the egg so that it's spread evenly across the pan.

4. When the egg is half-cooked, use large chopsticks to roll up the omelet, starting on the front side of the pan.

5. Apply a thin layer of oil in the empty space of the pan.

6. Add another ¼ to ⅓ of the egg mixture to the empty part of the pan.

7. Lift up the cooked egg with the chopsticks and tip the pan so the new egg mixture flows underneath it, covering the whole pan.

8. When the rest of the egg mixture is mostly cooked, but still slightly runny, roll the egg back towards you.

9. Continue to roll the cooked egg mixture to one side of the pan, add more oil, and then add the rest of the egg mixture until finished.

菜箸1本を
さし込むと
巻きやすい

Inserting a large chopstick makes it easy to roll.

🍥 クッキングメモ / COOKING MEMO

卵のとき方が肝心

卵をとくときは、まず菜箸で白身を4〜5回つまみ上げて切り、菜箸でボウルの底をこするように左右に動かして泡立てないように手早くまぜるのがポイント。ときすぎるとこしがなくなってしまいます。あとはプロセスどおりに焼いていくと「だし巻き卵」の完成。形よくできなかったときは、熱いうちにペーパータオルやラップに包んで、形をととのえればだいじょうぶです。

It's important how you mix the eggs

When you mix the eggs, first lift up the egg whites four or five times with the large chopsticks, and move the chopsticks back and forth along the bottom of the bowl. Stirring the eggs quickly but without making it foam up is key. If you over-mix the eggs, the liquid will lose body. Beyond that, follow the recipe, and you'll get a finished Japanese omelet. If the omelet's shape doesn't come out as well as desired, wrap the omelet in a paper towel or plastic wrap while it's still hot to fix the shape.

千草焼き
SAUTÉED CHIGUSA

炒めた野菜を卵液に加えて、あせらずに弱火でじっくり焼きます。
Add the sautéed vegetables to the egg mixture and sauté slowly over low heat.

220 kcal

1人分
One serving

材料（2人分）

卵		3個
えのきだけ		1袋
にんじん		小½本
さやいんげん		50g
ごま油		小さじ1(5ml)
A	酒	大さじ1 (15ml)
	砂糖	小さじ½(2.5ml)
	塩	少々
B	砂糖	大さじ1 (15ml)
	みりん	大さじ1 (15ml)
	しょうゆ	大さじ½ (7.5ml)
サラダ油		適宜

作り方

1. にんじんは2cm長さのせん切り、いんげんは斜め薄切り、えのきは根元を落とし、2cm長さに切ってほぐす。

2. フライパンにごま油を熱して①の野菜を炒める。Aで調味し、汁けを残さないように炒めて冷ます。

3. 卵をときほぐして、Bの砂糖、みりん、しょうゆで調味し、②の野菜を加える。

4. 卵焼きなべにサラダ油を熱し、卵液を流し入れる。ふたをして弱火で10〜12分焼く。

5. 表面が流れなくなったら、卵焼きなべを火からおろしてふたごとひっくり返し、卵焼きなべをそっとはずす。

6. 卵をそっと卵焼きなべにすべり込ませて戻し入れる。再び火にかけて焼き上げ、食べやすく切る。

にらじゃこ入り卵焼き

GARLIC CHIVES AND JAKO OMELET

Ingredients (2 servings)

3 eggs
1 bag enoki mushrooms
½ small carrot
50g green beans
1 tsp (5ml) sesame oil

A | 1 tbsp (15ml) sake
½ tsp (2.5ml) sugar
Salt, to your taste

B | 1 tbsp (15ml) sugar
1 tbsp (15ml) mirin
(sweet sake)
½ tbsp (7.5ml) soy sauce

Salad oil, as needed

Directions

1. Cut the carrot into 2cm strips, and cut the green beans into thin diagonal pieces. Take off the bottom of the enoki mushrooms and cut them into 2cm lengths and separate.

2. Heat the sesame oil in a frying pan and sauté the vegetables from 1. Add the A seasonings, sauté until no water is left, and set aside to cool.

3. Stir the eggs, add the sugar, mirin and soy sauce from B, and add the vegetables from 2.

4. Heat the salad oil in an omelet pan and add the egg mixture. Cover with a lid and cook over low heat for 10 to 12 minutes.

5. When the surface is no longer runny, take the omelet pan off the heat, flip it over and gently remove the omelet pan.

6. Gently slide the omelet back into the pan. Cook the omelet on the new side and cut it into bite-size pieces.

にらとじゃこで味も栄養も充実。
The garlic chives and jako make this omelet both rich in taste and nutrition.

231 kcal
1人分
One serving

材料（2人分）

卵‥‥‥‥‥‥‥‥‥‥‥‥‥‥‥4個
にら‥‥‥‥‥‥‥‥‥‥‥½束（50g）
ちりめんじゃこ‥‥‥‥‥‥‥‥10g

A | 酒‥‥‥‥‥‥‥‥小さじ1（5ml）
しょうゆ‥‥‥小さじ½（2.5ml）
塩‥‥‥‥‥‥‥‥‥‥‥‥‥少々

サラダ油‥‥‥‥‥‥大さじ1（15ml）
紅しょうが‥‥‥‥‥‥‥‥‥‥適宜

作り方

1. にらはこまかく刻む。じゃこは熱湯を回しかけて湯をきる。

2. 卵をときほぐしてAで調味し、にら、じゃこを加えてさっとまぜる。

3. フライパンを熱してサラダ油をなじませ、卵液の⅓量を流し入れる。あとは、だし巻き卵（p.166）と同様に巻き込んで焼く。

4. 食べやすく切って器に盛り、紅しょうがを添える。

Ingredients (2 servings)

4 eggs
½ bunch (50g) garlic chives
10g dried baby jako sardines

A | 1 tsp (5ml) sake
½ tsp (2.5ml) soy sauce
Salt, to your taste

1 tbsp (15ml) salad oil
Pickled ginger, as needed

Directions

1. Chop the chives finely. Blanch the sardines by pouring hot water in circles over them and drain.

2. Mix the eggs and add the chives, sardines and A seasonings. Mix them lightly.

3. Heat a frying pan and add salad oil. Add ⅓ of the egg mixture. Cook the omelet as described in the recipe for Japanese omelet (see page 166).

4. Cut into bite-size pieces and serve with pickled ginger.

卵・豆腐・その他
Eggs, Tofu and More

茶わん蒸し
CHAWANMUSHI (STEAMED EGG CUSTARD)

卵液を一度こしてから蒸すと、仕上がりが断然違います。
It makes a big difference if the egg is strained once before steaming.

112 kcal
1人分
One serving

材料(2人分)

卵 ························· 1個
えび ······················ 6尾
かまぼこ ···················· 2cm
しめじ ···················· ½パック

A だし ·········· 1カップ (200ml)
　酒 ············· 小さじ1 (5ml)
　砂糖 ········· 小さじ½ (2.5ml)
　塩 ·········· 小さじ¼ (1.25ml)
　しょうゆ ······· 小さじ½ (2.5ml)

B 酒 ············· 小さじ1 (5ml)
　塩 ······················ 少々

三つ葉 ···················· 少々

作り方

1. Aのだしを人肌程度にあたため、酒、砂糖、塩、しょうゆで調味しておく。

2. えびは背わたを抜きとって殻をむき（尾と、尾のつけ根の1節を残す）、Bの下味をつけておく。

3. かまぼこは5mm厚さに切り、しめじは石づきを切りとって、ほぐす。

4. 卵をときほぐして、①を加えまぜる。

5. 卵液を万能こし器でなめらかにこす。

6. フライパンの深さと同じくらいの背の低い耐熱容器に具を入れ、卵液を静かに注ぎ入れる。

7. フライパンにふきんを敷いて湯を1cm深さまで注ぐ。容器を入れてふたをし、弱火で13〜14分蒸す。

8. 竹ぐしを刺してみて、澄んだ汁が上がってくるようなら蒸し上がり。3cm長さに切った三つ葉をあしらう。

Ingredients (2 servings)

1 egg
6 shrimps
2cm kamaboko
½ pack shimeji mushrooms

A | 1 cup (200ml) soup stock
| 1 tsp (5ml) sake
| ½ tsp (2.5ml) sugar
| ¼ tsp (1.25ml) salt
| ½ tsp (2.5ml) soy sauce

B | 1 tsp (5ml) sake
| Salt, to your taste

Mitsuba trefoil, to your taste

Directions

1. Warm the soup stock in A to body temperature and add the sake, sugar, salt and soy sauce.

2. De-vein the shrimp and remove the shell, but leave the tail and the last shell segment. Add the B seasonings.

3. Slice the kamaboko into 5mm pieces. Cut off the hard bottoms of the shimeji mushrooms and separate them.

4. Beat the eggs and mix into the soup stock in 1.

5. Strain the egg mixture with an strainer until smooth.

6. Add the other ingredients to a heat-resistant bowl with sides as low as that of a frying pan and gently add the egg mixture.

7. Lay a cloth at the bottom of a frying pan and add hot water to a depth of 1 cm. Place the bowls in the frying pan and cover. Steam over low heat for 13 to 14 minutes.

8. Poke the chawanmushi with a bamboo skewer. If clear broth rises up, it's done. Garnish with mitsuba trefoil cut into 3cm lengths.

ふたにも
ふきんを
かけて結ぶ
Tie the ends of the towel across the top of the lid.

ひと手間
かけてなめらか
仕上げに
It takes a little extra work, but the smooth results are worth it.

♨ クッキングメモ / COOKING MEMO

フライパンで簡単!

蒸し器がなくてもだいじょうぶ。フライパンでおいしい茶わん蒸しが作れます。ただし、少人数向きなので4人分なら2回に分けて。もちろん蒸し器で蒸してもOKです。蒸すときは強火で蒸すと、すが立ちやすいので弱火で蒸します。湯げがふたにたまってしずくが落ちないように、乾いたふきんをはさむのも忘れずに。

It's easy to make chawanmushi using a frying pan!

Chawanmushi doesn't require a steamer. It's easy to make using just a frying pan. This method can only be used to make two servings, so follow the recipe twice to make four servings. Of course, you can also use a steamer. Bubbles tend to form when steamed over high heat, so it's best to use low heat. Lay a dry towel under the lid to prevent the condensed steam from dripping into the bowls.

肉豆腐
TOFU AND MEAT

おなじみの肉豆腐に、ビタミンCたっぷりの赤ピーマンを加えて、新しいおいしさ発見!
Add red bell peppers full of vitamin C to a familiar tofu and meat dish for a new taste!

407 kcal

1人分
One serving

水っぽく
仕上がらないように
This is to avoid making
the tofu watery.
→

材料（2人分）

木綿豆腐 ···················· 1丁
牛こまぎれ肉 ················ 150g
ねぎ ························· 2本
赤ピーマン ··················· ½個
ごま油 ··············· 大さじ½（7.5ml）

A | 酒 ············· ¼カップ（50ml）
　 | 湯 ············· 1カップ（200ml）
　 | 砂糖 ··········· 大さじ½（7.5ml）
　 | しょうゆ ········· 大さじ1（15ml）

万能ねぎ ····················· 5本

作り方

1. 豆腐は一口大に切ってざるに入れ、
   20～30分おいて水切りする。

2. ねぎは3cm長さのぶつ切りにする。
   赤ピーマンは乱切り、万能ねぎは
   小口切りにする。

3. フライパンにごま油を熱して牛肉を
   炒める。肉の色が変わり始めたら、
   ねぎを加えて炒める。

4. ねぎにこんがりと焼き色がついたら、
   Aの酒、湯、砂糖、しょうゆの順に
   加えて調味する。

5. 煮立ったら弱めの中火にして、アク
   をていねいにとる。

6. 豆腐を加えてときどきまぜ、15～16
   分煮る。汁けがなくなったらピーマン
   を加えて一煮し、万能ねぎを散らす。

Ingredients (2 servings)

1 block firm tofu
150g thinly-cut beef
2 naganegi onions
½ red bell pepper
½ tbsp (7.5ml) sesame oil

A | ¼ cup (50ml) sake
　 | 1 cup (200ml) hot water
　 | ½ tbsp (7.5ml) sugar
　 | 1 tbsp (15ml) soy sauce

5 banno-negi onions

Directions

1. Cut the tofu into bite-size cubes and set in a strainer to drain for 20 to 30 minutes.

2. Chop the naganegi onion into 3cm lengths. Roughly chop the red bell pepper and chop the banno-negi onions into small pieces.

3. Heat the sesame oil in a pan and sauté the beef. When the meat begins to change color, add the naganegi onions.

4. When the onion is browned, season with the sake, hot water, sugar, and soy sauce in A, in that order.

5. When it starts to boil, turn to medium-low heat and carefully remove the scum.

6. Add the tofu and simmer for 15 to 16 minutes, stirring occasionally. When the liquid has evaporated, add the bell pepper. Sprinkle in the banno-negi when it comes to a boil again.

↖
火を少し弱めるとアクをとりやすい
The scum is easy to remove
if you turn down the heat
a little.

豆腐ステーキ・肉みそかけ
TOFU STEAK AND MISO PORK

ごま油でこんがりと香ばしく焼いた豆腐に甘辛い肉みそをのせて、ボリュームアップ。
Aromatic baked tofu with sesame oil, topped with salty-sweet miso pork to add volume.

409 kcal
1人分
One serving

材料（2人分）

木綿豆腐	1丁
豚ひき肉	80g
ねぎ	10cm
しょうが	1かけ
ごま油	大さじ1 (15ml)
A 酒	大さじ3 (45ml)
砂糖	大さじ3 (45ml)
みそ	大さじ4 (60ml)
パセリ	少々

作り方

1. 豆腐は横半分に切り、さらに厚みを半分に切ってざるに入れ、水きりする。

2. ねぎ、しょうがはみじん切りにする。

3. ごま油大さじ½ (7.5ml)を熱し、ねぎ、しょうがを炒める。香りが立ったらひき肉を加えてほぐすように炒める。

4. Aの酒、砂糖、みそを加えて調味し、よくまぜながら軽く煮詰める。

5. ごま油大さじ½ (7.5ml)を熱し、豆腐の両面をこんがりと焼く。器に盛り、④の肉みそをのせてパセリを添える。

🔍 クッキングメモ

調理は「段取りよく」が基本

豆腐は厚みがあると中まで火が通りにくいので、厚みを半分に切って、水きりはしっかりと。水きりしている間に、段取りよく肉みその準備をすれば時間のロスもありません。ここでは、肉みそに豚ひき肉を使っていますが、あっさりと仕上げたいなら、鶏ひき肉で作ってもおいしいです。

Ingredients (2 servings)

1 block firm tofu
80g ground pork
10cm naganegi onion
1 piece ginger
1 tbsp (15ml) sesame oil

A | 3 tbsp (45ml) sake
　 | 3 tbsp (45ml) sugar
　 | 4 tbsp (60ml) miso

Parsley, to your taste

Directions

1. Cut the tofu in half horizontally, cut again into 4 equal pieces and drain in a strainer.

2. Mince the naganegi onion and ginger.

3. Heat $\frac{1}{2}$ tbsp (7.5ml) of sesame oil in the pan, and sauté the ginger and naganegi onion. When the spices release their aroma, add the ground pork and break the clumps.

4. Add mixture A (sake, sugar, and miso). Simmer gently while stirring well.

5. Heat $\frac{1}{2}$ tbsp (7.5ml) of sesame oil and brown the tofu on both sides. Serve on a plate and top with the ground pork from 4. Garnish with parsley.

🔍 COOKING MEMO

Planning is one of the basics of skillful cooking.

If tofu is too thick, it won't be cooked all the way through, so cut it in half sideways and drain thoroughly. While the tofu is draining, save time by preparing the ground pork. In this recipe, ground pork is mixed with miso. For a lighter dish, minced chicken is also delicious.

いり豆腐
IRI-DOFU (SCRAMBLED TOFU)

最後に卵でまとめるのは、豆腐をパラリとさせる大切なプロセス。
Finishing up with the egg is an important step that gives the tofu a crumb-like texture.

282 kcal
1人分
One serving

材料 (2人分)

木綿豆腐 ………………………… 1丁
にんじん ……………… 小½本 (50g)
干ししいたけ (もどす) …………… 2個
えび ……………………………… 5尾
サラダ油 ………… 大さじ½ (7.5ml)

A | だし ……………… ¼カップ (50ml)
　 | 酒 ……………… 大さじ2 (30ml)
　 | 砂糖 …………… 小さじ2 (10ml)
　 | みりん ………… 大さじ1 (15ml)
　 | 塩 …………… 小さじ¼ (1.25ml)
　 | しょうゆ ……… 小さじ2 (10ml)

卵 ……………………………… 1個
青のり ………………………… 少々

作り方

1. 豆腐は手でくずし、ざるに入れて水きりする。

2. にんじん、しいたけは1cm角に切る。えびは背わたを抜きとり、殻をむいて同じくらいの大きさに切る。

3. サラダ油を熱し、強火でにんじん、しいたけ、えびを炒める。豆腐を加えて炒め合わせる。

4. 全体に油が回ったらAで調味し、汁けをとばすようにいり煮する。

5. とき卵を回し入れてさっとまぜて火を通す。器に盛り、青のりを散らす。

🔍 クッキングメモ

**あり合わせの材料で
気軽に作れる**

手作りならではのおいしさが伝わる「いり豆腐」は、表面に穴があって甘みが濃縮された木綿豆腐がおすすめ。野菜とうまみの出る材料はにんじん、しいたけ、えびのほかに、さやいんげん、絹さや、三つ葉、あさりのむき身、桜えび、鶏ひき肉、きくらげなど。

Ingredients (2 servings)

1 block firm tofu
½ small carrot (50g)
2 dried shiitake mushrooms
5 shrimps
½ tbsp (7.5ml) salad oil

A | ¼ cup (50ml) soup stock
　 | 2 tbsp (30ml) sake
　 | 2 tsp (10ml) sugar
　 | 1 tbsp (15ml) mirin (sweet sake)
　 | ¼ tsp (1.25ml) salt
　 | 2 tsp (10ml) soy sauce

1 egg
Ao-nori green laver flakes, to your taste

Directions

1. Crumble the tofu with your hands and drain in a strainer.

2. Dice the carrot and shiitake mushrooms into 1cm cubes. De-vein the shrimps, peel and cut into similar sizes.

3. Heat the salad oil over high heat and stir-fry the carrots, shiitake mushrooms and shrimp. Add the tofu and stir-fry together.

4. When the oil has been absorbed, season with A and allow the broth to evaporate.

5. Pour in the beaten egg in circles, mix and heat through. Place on a serving dish and sprinkle the green laver.

← 余分な水分はとばしてポロポロに
Dry out the excess water to make it crumbly.

🔍 COOKING MEMO

A dish you can make with almost any ingredient

The homemade taste of iri-dofu (scrambled tofu) goes best with firm tofu, which has holes on the surface and a heavy sweetness. Vegetables and other ingredients that make for a good flavor are carrots, shiitake mushrooms, shrimp, green beans, snow peas, mitsuba trefoil, clam meat, sakura-ebi shrimp, ground chicken meat, cloud ear mushrooms, etc.

揚げ出し豆腐
DEEP-FRIED TOFU

なめらかな舌ざわりの絹ごし豆腐をふっくらと色よく揚げて、熱いところにだしのきいたかけ汁を。
Smooth-textured tofu, lightly fried to a nice color, then covered and served with a rich soup stock while piping hot.

202 kcal

1人分
One serving

材料（2人分）

絹ごし豆腐 ……………………… 1丁
大根 ……………………………… 適宜

A だし ……………¾カップ（150ml）
　 塩 …………………………………少々
　 しょうゆ …………小さじ2（10ml）
　 みりん ……………小さじ1（5ml）

かたくり粉 ……………………………適宜
揚げ油 …………………………………適宜
あさつきの小口切り……………………少々
おろししょうが …………………………少々

作り方

1. 豆腐はペーパータオルでぴったり包む。斜めにした台にのせて皿で重しをし、20〜25分水きりする。

2. 大根はおろして茶こし（またはざる）に入れ、自然に水きりする。

3. なべにAのだし、塩、しょうゆ、みりんを合わせ、一煮立ちさせる。

4. 豆腐を半分に切ってかたくり粉を全体にまんべんなくまぶし、余分な粉をはたき落とす。

5. 揚げ油を170〜180度に熱して豆腐をカラリと揚げる。熱いかけ汁をかけ、大根おろし、薬味をあしらう。

🔍 クッキングメモ

豆腐の水きりは重要ポイント

豆腐は皿などの重しをのせて水きりします。水きりの時間が短いと仕上がりも水っぽく、油はねの原因にも。逆に、皿が重すぎたり、時間を長くおきすぎると豆腐がかたくなってまずくなります。豆腐は適度に水けを含んで、ふっくらとやわらかいほうがおいしいので20〜25分を目安に。

斜めにしておくと水が流れ落ちる
If you leave it tilted, the water will drain out of the tofu.

Ingredients (2 servings)

1 block silken tofu
Daikon radish, as needed

A ¾ cup (150ml) soup stock
　 Salt, to your taste
　 2 tsp (10ml) soy sauce
　 1 tsp (5ml) mirin (sweet sake)

Potato starch, as needed
Frying oil, as needed
Finely chopped asatsuki chives, to your taste
Grated ginger, to your taste

Directions

1. Firmly wrap the tofu with a paper towel. Place it on a tilted surface and put a plate on it. Let the water drain out for 20 to 25 minutes.

2. Grate the daikon radish and place in a tea strainer (or a strainer) to drain the water.

3. Put the soup stock, salt, soy sauce, and mirin from A into a pot and boil.

4. Cut the tofu in half and cover in starch. Dust off the excess starch.

5. Heat the frying oil to between 170 and 180 degrees. Deep-fry the tofu. Pour the soup stock over it and top with the grated daikon radish and spices.

🔍 COOKING MEMO

The key is to drain the tofu

Drain the tofu by placing a plate or other weight on it. The tofu will turn out watery if it is only drained for a short time, and the moisture will also cause the oil to sputter. On the other hand, if the plate is too heavy or you leave the tofu to drain for too long, the tofu will get hard and not taste as good. The light and fluffy tofu tastes best when it is moderately drained for about 20 to 25 minutes.

卵・豆腐・その他 Eggs, Tofu and More

絹さやとにんじんの白あえ

SNOW PEAS AND CARROT SHIRA-AE

豆腐とごまを衣にしたあえ物です。なめらかな食感に自然の甘みが加わります。
A tofu and sesame seed marinated dish. It has added natural sweetness and a smooth texture.

110 kcal
1人分
One serving

材料（2人分）

絹ごし豆腐……………⅓丁（100g）
絹さや………………………30g
にんじん………………½本（70g）
こんにゃく…………………………½枚

A｜だし…………½カップ（100ml）
　｜砂糖……………小さじ1（5ml）
　｜塩………………………少々

B｜砂糖……………小さじ2（10ml）
　｜塩……………小さじ¼（1.25ml）
　｜あたりごま（白）… 大さじ1（15ml）

作り方

1. 豆腐はくずして、2枚重ねたペーパータオルに包んで軽くしぼり、水きりする。

2. 絹さやは筋をとって斜め半分に切り、熱湯でさっとゆでて湯をきる。

3. にんじんは細切り、こんにゃくは細切りにして下ゆでし、からいりする。Aで汁けを残さないように煮る。

4. すり鉢に豆腐を入れてすりつぶし、Bを加えてすりまぜる。

5. 絹さや、汁けを軽くきったにんじん、こんにゃくを加えてあえる。

香ばしくなめらかに
すりまぜる
Grind until it's smooth and savory.

🔍 クッキングメモ

あたりごまで風味よく

あえ物の衣などに使うあたりごまは、自分で作ると作りたての風味を楽しめます。弱火でゆっくりとからいりしたごまが丸くふくらんできたら1粒つまみ、ひねってつぶれたらすり鉢にあけ、油が出るようになるまでなめらかにすります。

少量なら手軽にできるこの方法で
This is easy to do with a small amount.

Ingredients (2 servings)

⅓ block silken tofu (100g)
30g snow peas
½ carrot (70g)
½ block konnyaku

A｜ ½ cup (100ml) soup stock
　｜ 1 tsp (5ml) sugar
　｜ Salt, to your taste

B｜ 2 tsp (10ml) sugar
　｜ ¼ tsp (1.25ml) salt
　｜ 1 tbsp (15ml) ground white sesame

Directions

1. Break up the tofu and drain by using two sheets of paper towel to wrap and squeeze lightly.

2. Remove the stalky part of the snow peas and cut into halves diagonally. Blanch in boiling water and drain.

3. Slice the carrots and konnyaku into thin pieces, then boil. Stir until all the water evaporates. Add A and simmer until there isn't any liquid.

4. Put the tofu into a suri-bachi (Japanese grinding bowl) and grind. Add the ingredients in B and grind together.

5. Add the snow peas, lightly-drained carrots and konnyaku, and marinate.

🔍 COOKING MEMO

Flavor with ground sesame

You can marinate using your freshly ground sesame for a fragrant taste. When the slow-roasted sesame seeds become plump, squeeze one of the seeds. If you are able to smash it, put the seeds in a suri-bachi grinding bowl and grind until it becomes oily and smooth.

卵・豆腐・その他
Eggs, Tofu and More

こんにゃくのおかか煮

KONNYAKU WITH SHAVED BONITO

こんにゃくはだしとしょうゆで煮て歯ごたえよく仕上げます。
The konnyaku is cooked in soup stock and soy sauce for a chewy finish.

Ingredients (2 servings)

1 block konnyaku
2 packets shaved dried bonito (10g)

A | 1 cup (200ml) soup stock
  | 1 tbsp (15ml) soy sauce

Directions

1. Cut the konnyaku into 5mm thick pieces, starting from the side. Pour enough water to cover and boil over high heat for 1 to 2 minutes. Drain the water.

2. Put the konnyaku in a pot and heat over high heat. Stir around with large chopsticks to get rid of the moisture.

3. Add the ingredients in A and season, then heat over medium heat for 20 to 25 minutes. Stir occasionally until there is no more liquid. Turn the heat off, serve and top with the dried bonito.

30 kcal
1人分
One serving

POINTER

下ゆでしたこんにゃくは、からいりして水分を完全にとばします。こうすることで、調味料を加えたときに味の含みがよくなります。

Allow all the moisture in the pre-boiled konnyaku to evaporate. That way, when you add the seasoning, the flavors will blend in better.

材料 (2人分)

こんにゃく･･･････････････････1枚
削りがつお･･････････････2袋 (10g)

A | だし･･･････1 カップ(200ml)
  | しょうゆ･･････大さじ1 (15ml)

作り方

1. こんにゃくは端から5mm厚さに切る。なべに入れてかぶるくらいの水を注ぎ、強火にかけて1～2分下ゆでして、湯をきる。

2. なべにこんにゃくを入れて強火にかけ、菜箸でまぜながら水分をとばすようにからいりする。

3. Aを加えて調味し、中火にしてときどきまぜ、ほとんど汁けがなくなるまで20～25分煮る。火を止めて削りがつおをまぶす。

しらたきのたらこ煮

SHIRATAKI AND SALTED COD ROE

しらたきをほんのり桜色に。たらこのうまみに、食感の楽しさをプラスして。

Salted cod roe will make the shirataki turn into the pink color of cherry blossoms and give it an appetizing flavor.

57 kcal
1人分
One serving

Ingredients (2 servings)

1 bag shirataki

2 piece salted cod roe

A | 1 cup (200ml) soup stock
1 tsp (5ml) sugar
Salt, to your taste
½ tbsp (7.5ml) soy sauce

Directions

1. Roughly chop the shirataki. Blanch in boiling water for 1 or 2 minutes and put into a strainer to drain the water. Put it back into a pot and let it dry out.

2. Place the salted cod roe on a sheet of plastic wrap and break it up. Remove the remaining thin layer of skin by scraping gently with a spoon.

3. Combine the ingredients in A in a pot. When it comes to a boil, add the shirataki and cook. Stir occasionally. When there is no more liquid left, toss the salted cod roe over the shirataki.

完全に水分をとばす

Allow all the moisture to evaporate.

材料（2人分）

しらたき・・・・・・・・・・・・・・・・・・・・・1袋
たらこ・・・・・・・・・・・・・・・・・・・・・・・・1腹

A | だし・・・・・・・・・1カップ（200ml）
砂糖・・・・・・・・・ 小さじ1 (5ml)
塩・・・・・・・・・・・・・・・・・・・・・・少々
しょうゆ・・・・・・ 大さじ½ (7.5ml)

作り方

1. しらたきはざっと刻んで、煮立った湯に入れて1〜2分ゆでてざるに上げ、なべに戻してからいりする。

2. ラップを敷いてたらこをのせ、スプーンでこそげて薄皮をとり除く。

3. Aを合わせ、煮立ったらしらたきを入れて煮る。ときどきまぜ、汁けがなくなったらたらこを全体にまぶす。

大豆の五目煮
STEWED SOYBEAN MIX

なべに入れてやわらかく煮ます。
Cook the beans in a pot until they are soft.

389 kcal
1人分
One serving

Ingredients (2 servings)

150g soybeans (dried)
½ small carrot
¼ burdock
2 pieces dried shiitake mushrooms
1 10cm long kobu seaweed

A | ¼ tsp (1.25ml) salt
  | 1 tbsp (15ml) soy sauce
  | 1.5 tbsp (22.5ml) mirin (sweet sake)

Directions

1. Rinse the soybeans, add three times the amount of water and leave to soak overnight. Transfer the soybeans with the soaking water into a pot and boil until tender.

2. Cut the carrot and burdock into 1cm cubes and soak the burdock in water. Soak the shiitake and kobu in water and cut into 1cm cubes.

3. Put all the ingredients in 2 and A into the pot in 1. Stirring occasionally, cook on low heat until most of the liquid has evaporated.

材料 (2人分)

大豆（乾）・・・・・・・・・・・・・・・・・・・150g
にんじん・・・・・・・・・・・・・・・・・・小½本
ごぼう・・・・・・・・・・・・・・・・・・・・・¼本
干ししいたけ・・・・・・・・・・・・・・・・2個
昆布・・・・・・・・・・・・10cm長さを1枚

A | 塩・・・・・・・・・・小さじ¼ (1.25ml)
  | しょうゆ・・・・・・・・大さじ1 (15ml)
  | みりん・・・・・大さじ1.5 (22.5ml)

作り方

1. 大豆はさっと洗って3倍量の水に一晩つけてもどす。もどし汁ごとなべに移し、やわらかくなるまでゆでる。

2. にんじん、ごぼうは1cm角に切り、ごぼうは水にさらす。しいたけ、昆布はもどして1cm角に切る。

3. ①のなべに②の材料とAを加え、弱火でときどきまぜてほとんど汁けがなくなるまで煮る。

指でつまんで
ゆでかげんをみる
Check the
doneness with
your fingers.

きんとき豆の甘煮
SWEETENED RED KIDNEY BEANS

豆がやわらかくなってから調味しましょう。
Season after the beans get soft.

382 kcal

1人分
One serving

Ingredients (2 servings)

150g red kidney beans (dried)
70g sugar
Salt, to your taste

Directions

1. Rinse the beans, pour in 3 cups (600ml) of water and leave overnight.

2. Along with the soaking water, transfer the beans into a pot and bring to a boil over high heat. Drain.

3. Cover the beans with water and heat once again. Once it starts to boil, heat over medium heat for 20 to 30 minutes, removing the scum.

4. Add the sugar once the beans get soft. Cook over low heat for 15 to 20 minutes to soak in the sweetness and finish by adding salt, and bring to a final boil.

POINTER

豆をゆでるときはゆで汁から豆が出るとやわらかく煮えないので、かぶった状態になるように水を足しながらゆでます。

When you are boiling the beans, they won't turn out tender if they are exposed above the water. Make sure there is enough water to cover the beans when they are boiling. You can add water if there isn't enough.

材料（2人分）

きんとき豆（乾）‥‥‥‥‥ 150g
砂糖 ‥‥‥‥‥‥‥‥‥‥‥ 70g
塩 ‥‥‥‥‥‥‥‥‥‥‥‥ 少々

作り方

1. 豆はさっと洗って3カップ（600ml）の水に一晩つけてもどす。

2. もどし汁ごとなべに移し、強火にかけて煮立ったら湯をきる。

3. かぶるくらいの水を加えて再び火にかける。煮立ったら中火にしてアクをとり、20〜30分ゆでる。

4. 豆がやわらかくなったら砂糖を加える。弱火で15〜20分煮て甘みを含ませ、仕上げに塩を加えて一煮する。

卵・豆腐・その他
Eggs, Tofu and More

185

切り干し大根のいり煮
STIR-FRIED DAIKON RADISH STRIPS

もどした切り干し大根を使って。
Use reconstituted the dried daikon radish strips.

166 kcal
1人分
One serving

Ingredients (2 servings)

40g dried daikon radish strips
1 slice abura-age (deep-fried tofu)
1 red hot pepper
½ tbsp (7.5ml) sesame oil

A | 2 cups (400ml) soup stock
1 tbsp (15ml) mirin (sweet sake)
2 tsp (10ml) soy sauce
½ tsp (2.5ml) salt

Directions

1. Wash the dried daikon radish strips thoroughly with lots of water, and then repeat 2 or 3 times.

2. Soak in just enough water to cover for 20 to 25 minutes, and then wring out all the water.

3. Put the abura-age in a strainer and pour hot water over it to remove oil. Drain and cut in half lengthwise, then cut into thin pieces.

4. Soak the red pepper in lukewarm water so it reconstitutes, then remove the seeds and cut into small pieces.

5. Heat sesame oil in a pan and cook 2, 3, and 4. When the ingredients have been cooked through, add A and simmer for 18 to 20 minutes until there is no more liquid.

材料（2人分）

切り干し大根‥‥‥‥‥‥‥‥‥40g
油揚げ‥‥‥‥‥‥‥‥‥‥‥‥1枚
赤とうがらし‥‥‥‥‥‥‥‥‥1本
ごま油‥‥‥‥‥ 大さじ½ (7.5ml)

A | だし‥‥‥‥‥2カップ (400ml)
みりん‥‥‥‥ 大さじ1 (15ml)
しょうゆ‥‥‥‥ 小さじ2 (10ml)
塩‥‥‥‥‥‥ 小さじ½(2.5ml)

作り方

1. 切り干し大根はたっぷりの水でもみ洗いして水をかえ、これを2〜3回繰り返す。

2. ひたひたの水に20〜25分つけてもどし、水けをよくしぼる。

3. 油揚げはざるに入れ、熱湯をかけて油抜きする。湯をきって縦半分にし、細切りにする。

4. 赤とうがらしはぬるま湯につけてもどして種をとり、小口切りにする。

5. ごま油を熱して②〜④を炒める。油がなじんだらAを加え、ほとんど汁けがなくなるまで18〜20分煮る。

①  ②  ③  ④ ⑤

はりはり漬け
PICKLED DAIKON RADISH

切り干し大根は食物繊維の宝庫。
Dried daikon radish strips are a treasure trove of dietary fiber.

Ingredients (2 servings)

60g dried daikon radish strips
1 red hot pepper

A | 1 cup (200ml) soup stock
2 tbsp (30ml) soy sauce
4 tbsp (60ml) sugar
1.5 tsp (7.5ml) salt
½ cup (100ml) vinegar

Directions

1. Wash the dried daikon radish strips around in plenty of water while rubbing them. Change the water and repeat 2 to 3 times. Lightly submerge them in water for 7 to 8 minutes until they are reconstituted.

2. Remove the seeds from the red pepper and cut into small pieces.

3. Combine the red pepper and A (soup stock, soy sauce, sugar, and salt) in a pot and bring to a boil. Allow to cool and add vinegar to make vinaigrette.

4. Thoroughly wring and drain the daikon radish strips, and cover with the vinaigrette.

178 kcal
1人分
One serving

材料（2人分）

切り干し大根……………………60g
赤とうがらし……………………1本

A | だし………1 カップ(200ml)
しょうゆ………大さじ2 (30ml)
砂糖…………大さじ4 (60ml)
塩………小さじ1.5 (7.5ml)
酢…………½カップ(100ml)

作り方

1. 切り干し大根はたっぷりの水でもみ洗いして水をかえ、これを2〜3回繰り返す。ひたひたの水に7〜8分つけてもどす。

2. 赤とうがらしは種をとり、小口切りにする。

3. なべに赤とうがらし、Aのだし、しょうゆ、砂糖、塩を入れて一煮立ちさせ、冷めたら酢を加えて漬け汁を作る。

4. 切り干し大根の水けをよくしぼって、漬け汁に漬ける。

ひじきのいり煮

HIJIKI SEAWEED SALAD

ひじきはカルシウムや鉄分などを豊富に含んだヘルシー素材。
Hijiki is a healthy food rich in iron and calcium.

142 kcal

1人分
One serving

材料（2人分）

ひじき（乾燥）·····················30g
油揚げ·····························1枚
にんじん····························½本
こんにゃく··························½枚
ごま油···················大さじ½（7.5ml）

A | だし················2カップ（400ml）
  | みりん···············大さじ1（15ml）
  | しょうゆ··············小さじ1（5ml）
  | 塩················小さじ½（2.5ml）

作り方

1. ひじきはたっぷりの水に20〜25分つけてもどし、ざるに上げて水けをきる。

2. 油揚げは熱湯をかけて油抜きする。湯をきって縦半分にし、細切りにする。にんじんも細切りにする。

3. こんにゃくは細切りにして水を注ぎ、強火で1〜2分下ゆでする。

4. フライパンにごま油を熱して①〜③を炒める。水分がとんで油がなじんだらAを加えてときどきまぜ、ほとんど汁けがなくなるまで13〜15分煮る。

Ingredients (2 servings)

30g hijiki seaweed (dried)
1 piece abura-age (deep-fried tofu)
½ carrot
½ konnyaku
½ tbsp (7.5ml) sesame oil

A | 2 cups (400ml) soup stock
  | 1 tbsp (15ml) mirin (sweet sake)
  | 1 tsp (5ml) soy sauce
  | ½ tsp (2.5ml) salt

Directions

1. Reconstitute the hijiki in plenty of water for 20 to 25 minutes. Drain in a strainer.

2. Pour boiling water onto the abura-age to remove some of the oil. Drain the hot water and cut in half lengthwise. Slice into small strips. Slice the carrot into small strips as well.

3. Slice the konnyaku into small strips and cover with water. Boil over high heat for 1 to 2 minutes.

4. Heat sesame oil in a frying pan and sauté the items from 1 to 3. When the water evaporates and the oil has seeped in, add A and simmer. Stir occasionally and leave for 13 to 15 minutes until most of the liquid is gone.

POINTER

ひじきはたっぷりの水で洗って浮いた汚れや砂をとり除きます。もどすと4倍くらいになるので、たっぷりの水につけてもどします。

Wash the hijiki in plenty of water so the dirt and sand will float out. It will expand four times in size, so be sure to use enough water.

🔍 クッキングメモ

用途に合わせた味つけで

ひじきは食物繊維がたっぷり。油との相性が抜群なので、油揚げ、こんにゃく、にんじんを組み合わせて、ごま油でさっと炒めてからいり煮にすると、風味のよい仕上がりになります。火を止めてそのまま冷ますと味がよくなじみます。

🔍 COOKING MEMO

Flavored to match its purpose

Hijiki contains loads of dietary fiber, and it has excellent compatibility with oil. If it's cooked in sesame oil and combined with abura-age, konnyaku and carrots, it ends up with a delicious flavor. The flavor will deepen if you turn off the heat and allow it to cool. It can be stored if prepared using slightly strong seasonings.

卵・豆腐・その他
Eggs, Tofu and More

基本の味をマスターするための

計量の仕方

初めての料理はレシピどおりに調味料をきちんとはかることが、おいしい味つけの近道です。

The best way to master the dishes

How to measure

When making a dish for the first time, following the recipe and measuring the ingredients correctly is the most effective way to improve your cooking.

粉類をはかるときは	Measuring flour
### 小さじ1	### 1 teaspoon (tsp)
山盛りにすくいとり、すりきり棒やナイフなどで縁から表面を平らにして「すりきり」に（大さじ1も同様）。	Take a heaped spoonful and, with a stick or knife, level it off to make a correct measurement. (Do the same for 1 tbsp.)
### 小さじ½	### ½ teaspoon (tsp)
小さじ1をはかり、半分のところにラインを引いて目安をつけ、½量をとり除く（大さじ½も同様）。	Measure a tsp, then draw a line with your eyes for half and remove. (Do the same for ½ tbsp.)
### 小さじ⅓	### ⅓ teaspoon (tsp)
中心から3等分のラインを引き、一つ分を残してとり除く。⅔杯のときは二つ分残す。（大さじ⅓＝小さじ1）	Draw a line with your eyes for 3 equal parts and subtract, leaving one portion. When measuring two thirds, leave two portions. (⅓ tbsp = 1 tsp)
### 1カップ	### 1 cup
縁まで入って1カップのものはすりきりに。目盛りが縁より下のときはスプーンなどで、押さえつけないように表面を平らにする。	If the marking for the required amount is at the rim of the cup, level off at the top. When the marking for the desired amount is below the rim of the cup, use a spoon or similar object to level the surface without pressing down.

計量カップ
1 カップ= 200ml

Measuring cup
1 cup = 200ml

計量スプーン
大さじ1＝ 15ml　小さじ1＝ 5ml
＊小さじより小さい 2.5ml のさじがついていることもあるので注意。

Measuring spoon
1 tbsp=15 ml　1tsp=5ml
Check carefully because a smaller 2.5 ml tsp is often attached to the regular one.

手ばかり
手ばかりは不正確のようですが、同じ人の指先ではかる量は意外にばらつきがないものです。自分の指で感覚をつかんでいつもおいしい味に。

少々
塩、こしょう少々の目安は指ではかるなら、親指と人さし指でつまんだ量。容器からなら3〜5回ほど振り入れた量。

Measuring by hand
Hand measurement may seem inaccurate, but if the same person uses their fingertips, it is surprisingly consistent. Try to become familiar with how much you pinch with your fingers, and you'll soon be able to give dishes just the right flavor.

To your taste
When measuring a small amount of salt or pepper, pinch with your thumb and index finger. If you use a shaker, shake it 3 to 5 times to get the desired amount.

液体をはかるときは	Measuring liquids
### 小さじ1	### 1 teaspoon (tsp)
縁いっぱいに盛り上がるくらいに入れ、もう少しでこぼれ落ちるぎりぎりのところ（大さじ1も同様）。	Fill to the rim of the spoon, to the point where it is about to drip. (Do the same for 1 tbsp.) 
### 小さじ½	### ½ teaspoon (tsp)
底が丸くなっているので、スプーンの深さの⅔くらいまで入れると、ちょうど½杯（大さじ½も同様）。	The bottom of the spoon is round, so filling it up to two thirds will make half a teaspoon. (Do the same for ½ tbsp.) 
### 小さじ⅓	### ⅓ teaspoon (tsp)
底が丸くなっているので、スプーンの深さの半分くらいまで入れると、ちょうど⅓杯。（大さじ⅓＝小さじ1）	The bottom of the spoon is round, so filling up about half of it is equivalent to one third. (⅓ tbsp = 1 tsp)
### 1カップ	### 1 cup
水平なところにおいて液体を注ぎ入れる。目線が高かったり、低かったりすると正しい分量がはかれないので、必ず真横から目盛りを見ること。	Pour in the liquid on a flat surface. If you look at the level from a higher or lower point, you won't get the correct amount. Make sure you look at the graduation lines from the same height. 

検見﨑聡美 けんみざきさとみ

雑誌や書籍を中心に活躍中の料理研究家。管理栄養士。初心者でも手軽に作れる料理とセンスの良さには定評がある。著書は『絶対おいしい! はじめての楽しい料理』（主婦と生活社）、『1杯で確実に健康力アップ!みそ汁レシピ100』（主婦の友社）など多数。

Staff

装丁	鈴木住枝（Concent,Inc）
本文デザイン	金沢ありさ
英文作成	エートゥーゼット
撮影	梅澤 仁、中村 太
スタイリング	ダンノマリコ
熱量計算	橋本恵子
編集協力	大下康子
編集担当	町野慶美（主婦の友社）
英文校正	共同制作社

Special Thanks!

表紙の寿司写真協力／
梅丘寿司の美登利総本店
www.sushinomidori.co.jp
手頃な価格で外国人にも人気のお寿司屋さん。

新装版
英語でつくる基本の和食

編　者	主婦の友社
発行者	矢﨑謙三
発行所	株式会社主婦の友社
	〒101-8911
	東京都千代田区神田駿河台2-9
	電話 03-5280-7537（編集）
	03-5280-7551（販売）
印刷所	大日本印刷株式会社

©Shufunotomo Co., Ltd. 2016 Printed in Japan ISBN978-4-07-418260-2